Trans-nationalism and the Politics of Belonging

The debate on globalisation suggests that we live in a postnational world. *Trans-nationalism and the Politics of Belonging* challenges this notion, drawing attention to the continuing importance of the nation-state and the huge emotional investments in national identities. The authors argue that the increase in cross-border migration, though transnational in form, represents many vastly differing realities, from international commerce's wealthy jet-setters to the poor and dispossessed who are shunted from border to border in search of a safe place to make their home.

These ideas are explored through the following themes, using case studies from across the world:

* The experience of space and time ruptured by migration
* How migrants forge a sense of belonging in both national and transnational ways
* The ethnic and gendered relations of business enterprises, from the small-scale entrepreneurs to the global elite.

This book provides a fascinating and grounded insight into the everyday realities of diasporic lives in the global age.

Sallie Westwood is Professor of Sociology at Leicester University.
Annie Phizacklea is Professor of Sociology at Warwick University.

Trans-nationalism and the Politics of Belonging

Sallie Westwood and
Annie Phizacklea

London and New York

First published 2000 by Routledge
11 New Fetter Lane, London EC4P 4EE

Simultaneously published in the USA and Canada
by Routledge
29 West 35th Street, New York, NY 10001

Routledge is an imprint of the Taylor & Francis Group

© 2000 Sallie Westwood and Annie Phizacklea

Typeset in Perpetua by Taylor & Francis Books Ltd
Printed and bound in Great Britain by Clays Ltd, St Ives PLC

British Library Cataloguing in Publication Data
A catalogue record for this book is available from the British Library

Library of Congress Cataloguing in Publication Data
Westwood, Sallie.
    Trans-nationalism and the politics of belonging / Sallie Westwood and
    Annie Phizacklea.
    p. cm.
    Includes bibliographical references and index.
    1. Emigration and immigration. 2. Nationalism. 3. Ethnicity. I. Phizacklea,
    Annie. II. Title.
    JV6032.W48 2001
    320.54–dc21   00–042495

ISBN 0–415–18979–9 (hbk)
ISBN 0–415–18980–2 (pbk)

Contents

Acknowledgements

We would like to thank everyone who has been involved in the research for this book, particularly all the people we have interviewed over the years. We owe a special debt to the Economic and Social Research Council who have supported us financially for large parts of the research that we draw on here. Finally, we would like to thank Mari Shullaw for being a great editor.

Introduction

Trans-nationalism and the politics of belonging

Currently, there is considerable attention being paid to the phenomenon of globalisation. But when we reflected on the concept of globalisation within the context of our own research over the last ten years we realised that it pointed to the many contradictions and limitations of the concept. So we decided to put together a book which indicates an alternative view. We do not deny the importance of the activities and investment decisions of transnational companies, nor the revolution in transportation systems, and information and communication technologies, all of which have transformed the ordering of space and time in our lives and which all point to a postnationalist world. But we want to point you in a different direction, we want you to think about how the making of national identities is an ongoing process, not just in terms of the savagery of the Balkans or numerous other examples in the world today where 'ownership' of the nation-state is contested in brutal terms, but also in terms of the huge emotional, cultural and ideological investment that is made in order to forge a national identity amongst diverse peoples in Latin American states.

We also want you to think about who it is that benefits from processes of globalisation. It certainly is not the 'ragged army of the dispossessed' in Latin America, Asia or Africa who would like to share just a little of the benefits of globalisation. In our examination of contemporary migratory processes we hope to show how those who are fortunately geographically positioned in the contemporary, globalised world have built legal fortresses around themselves to keep the demonised 'other' out. Yet when we look at who these 'demons' are, they are usually well-educated, resourceful people who simply want to contribute to their family's well-being 'at home' or who have fled persecution there. In the latter part of the book we focus attention on these migrants who are not in a position to be termed 'transnationals' in its more limited usage, they are simply not in this league. Increasingly the term 'transnational' is being used to refer to the growing number of people who have the freedom, legally and economically, to move across borders and between cultures, doing business on their way. We do address this phenomenon in the book, but we are keen to alert the reader to the way in which these transnational business practices have been a way of life for many groups, such as Indian trading minorities, for centuries.

We use the term transnationalism in this book to draw attention to the two processes which are simultaneously at work. On the one hand the continuing importance of the nation and the emotional attachments invested in it, and on the other hand those processes such as cross-border migration which are transnational in form.

For many years we have been concerned with issues around migration, the economic, social and political realities of transnational communities and the making of national identities. Throughout this period we have been concerned to show how each of these processes is constituted in racialised, gendered and class relations which are by no means static, not least because of the ways in which individuals and collectivities contest certain boundaries and carve out new spaces of identity and control for themselves. In what follows we draw on ideas that have preoccupied our research agendas over the last decade, in the case of Sallie Westwood the formation of national identities and for Annie Phizacklea a concern with issues relating to women and migration. Part I of the book is written by Sallie Westwood and Part II by Annie Phizacklea. While our central concerns are different, we attempt to explore certain themes in both parts of the book; the first we have chosen to call 'Ruptures: race/space/time'; the second, 'The politics of belonging' and the final theme 'Economic ethnoscapes'. In so doing we hope to extend understandings of certain dimensions of the process of globalisation while indicating the limitations of the concept as well. We explore how a sense of belonging is forged in relation to national identities as well as the search for belonging and sense of identity in transnational communities and how the meaning of 'home' becomes stretched over time and space. Finally, we consider the gendered and ethnic relations of business enterprise from the harsh realities of the sweatshop and corner shop to the transnational entrepreneurs who increasingly pop up in the 'rich list' leagues of the world. It is perhaps when we move to the detail of what we term the economic ethnoscape that we can best understand the relationship between the global and the local and role of transnational communities within those spaces.

Ruptures: race/space/time

It was Stuart Hall who, over a decade ago, reminded us that 'we are all migrants now' (Hall, 1989) in a reference not only to the processes of the post-colonial migration of labour but to a postmodern world which is global in its concerns. This is a benign scenario of a psychic and social world in which the boundaries of modernist nation-states are transgressed and the pleasures of difference are celebrated. As an alternative Zygmunt Bauman (1998) presents a much less sanguine view of a globalised world in which the rich of the metropolitan core have become not Melucci's 'Nomads of the Western World' (Melucci, 1989) but tourists flying between destinations but always in the same hermetically sealed and carefully controlled environment of the international hotel with its bland surroundings and even more bland food. While the privileged consume other cultures integrated into the global economy as providers of holidays, sex, exotica and cheap labour, the poor world ravaged by a poverty, which is often the direct consequence of the international division of labour, is a ragged global army of the dispossessed at the gates of the rich white world which is determined to keep them out. This is a racialised scenario in which the poor are the impoverished of Africa, Asia and Latin America struggling to find a home. Bauman's broad strokes are not intended to be a simple description but a reminder in stark terms that the celebration of globalisation and migrancy is a narrative embedded in a specific white metropolitan world and is a very partial story.

The migrant, embodied and imagined, condenses our concerns with race, space and time and the politics of belonging. A figure, romanticised in popular culture from the songs of the Irish diaspora in Christy Moore's poetry and the sadness of the blues music of the African diaspora to the more recent hybrid popular forms of Apache Indian and Bally Sagoo in Britain and the Latino world of Maná in the US and

Carlos Vives from Colombia. In songs and consistently in writing, from
the Jewish-American novels of Malumud and Bellow to the work of
Richard Wright and Toni Morrison, fiction consistently tries to explore
the time–space frame within which psyches try to constitute a sense of
home. The poetics of exile, the pain of diasporic lives and the
celebration of hybridity in popular cultures across the globe are
curiously at odds with the ways in which sociologists and economists
have tried to conceptualise and analyse migration. There is, in fact, a
deep rupture between the poetic and experiential and the sociological
and economistic discourses which have sought to render migratory
processes intelligible.

Economists have been concerned with viewing individuals and then,
later, households as rational decision-making units as far as migration is
concerned. According to this economistic view households will weigh
up the costs and benefits of migration and act in such a way as to
maximise the benefits. Sociological accounts of migration have tended
to be located either within a political economy of migrant labour
approach or some form of structure and agency formulation with
structuration theory possibly being the most popular of these. In the
first instance the uneven development of capitalism leads to the out-
flow of people from the so-called periphery countries and their in-flow
to the metropolitan core as a source of cheap and vulnerable labour. In
the structuration approach, structural factors are not viewed as
necessarily external and constraining to the individual, they may be
enabling as individuals make and remake structures in the course of
their lives. We will see in the second part of this book how some
sociologists have applied these models. It is quite possible to draw on
each of these models and our past work sought not to refute the
importance of economic relations in the political economy approach
but to deconstruct some of the premises on which the model was built
and to privilege issues of racism and gender relations and the ways in
which they interact. Capitalism was constituted within processes of
racialisation, that is from the periods of enslavement through
indentured labour and into the current processes of the global supply
and demand for labour, capitalism in its formation and development
has been constituted as a racial formation (Winant, 1995). Capitalism
is not an abstract system, although it may be understood in an idealised
form. The production of commodities on a world scale involves both

racialised and gendered labour power. The movements of peoples around the world and the current competition among nations like India and the Philippines to be the supplier of the cheapest labour are part of the processes of racialisation. The story is further complicated by the movements of peoples within the newly capitalist nations like China where the greatest migrations of the twentieth century have been taking place over the last decade. The revamped version of migration in the notion of the new international division of labour sought ways in which to take account of the newly industrialising nations and the growing power of the Pacific rim which added to a view of migration not just from South to North but horizontally as well.

What is of interest in all these models is the way in which issues of time and space are central to their construction but become invisible. The models of migration build upon under-theorised notions of the spatial in sociology, historically constructed around a set of binaries — rural/urban, *Gemeinschaft/Gesellschaft*, traditional/modern and in relation to migration 'overthere and overhere'. It was this type of theorising that produced the distinction between developed and underdeveloped, first and third world. The point of departure for these characterisations was always the metropolitan core and in this sociology created its own 'others', who, on the whole, were then seen to be the preserve of anthropology with its colonial heritage coming to bear upon the migratory process. The consequences of these binaries was that incoming peoples were located as 'migrants' coming into 'host' societies as outsiders. This ensured that the citizenship conferred by the colonial order in the case of Britain and the cultural similarities with Britain were overlooked. There was no room in this framework for the notion of shared histories and cultures and the idea that the 'west and the rest', as Stuart Hall ironically called this binary, could be one and the same. Rather than concentrating on what the 'hosts' and the newcomers shared, attention focused on what separated them. An understanding of what is shared developed through cultural studies and generated an analysis of diasporic populations and cultures and hybridity, producing an account of Britishness which addresses whiteness as much as blackness or 'Asian-ness'. In part many of the understandings that have been developed have been crucially bound up with a revisioning of the role of space and spatiality in the production of social forms and the ways in which capitalist time has become increasingly compressed – Harvey's now famous time/space compression (1992). Central to these understandings has been the work of Lefebvre (1996) who conceives of space, not as a context, an empty stage on which social life takes place, but as infused with power relations which constitute social life. This view of spaces and sites is also developed in Foucault's work in which he elaborated the development of the institutional nexus of modern nation-states. But the economic is not entirely ignored, especially in relation to labour and its role, of special importance in this work in relation to migratory labour. Equally, Castells (1997) has brought together spatial relations with power flows and the ways in which forms of organising by social movements relate to resources in relation to places. He emphasised this as forms of collective consumption around which groups would organise, like women's groups in the poor barrios of Latin American cities who fought for land and water as the basis for survival.

Equally, attention to the issue of time has received a new focus following the work of Barbara Adam (1995) who has sought ways in which to dismantle the distinction between 'our' time and 'other' time, suggesting instead that throughout the world we live in a multiplicity of times. This is explored in the pages that follow, first of all in relation to the ways in which nations and national stories construct national time, the time of heroes and special events which bring the nation together if only temporarily and into which new members are inducted. This form of national time stays with people when they leave one nation-state and move to another as part of the migratory process. Instead, migrants celebrate national days from their home countries like those in New York from Colombia, or people of Irish descent throughout the Irish diaspora celebrating St Patrick's day. These are all forms of remembering which encourage people to think of home and provide a sense of belonging.

We have sought to understand the dynamic relations of people, cultures, economic processes and state formations as discontinuous, disruptive and in process and for this reason we use the term 'rupture' to describe the concerns of our first theme in the book. Changes in the ways of theorising migration, developments within ethnic relations and the contribution of cultural studies have produced a move away from the binary of strangers/host society to the study of diasporas, post-coloniality and transnationalism. In part our own work has contributed to this rupture while it simultaneously seeks to give centrality to the processes of racialisation, engendering and the theorisation of space and time.

The use of the plural term 'ruptures' signifies the extent to which we try in what follows to break with passive notions of migration between unitary nation-states and the idea of a linear movement from one place to another. Instead, the notion of rupture emphasises the active decision-making processes of migration and the ways in which economic and cultural phenomena are creatively reinscribed in new settings and the ways in which the diasporic feeds economically and culturally back into the homeland, for instance, through remittances. The use of the term rupture also suggests the unfinished and discontinuous nature of both the migratory process and the making of national identities and nations. For example, national identities are produced and reproduced in relation to a racialised/ethnicised conception of the national subject and citizen and this is reinforced through a claim to a specific space as territory which is presented as part of a national history (or time) into which nationals are inducted. At the same time the two chapters which explore the theme of rupture include a critique of overly simple views of globalisation. Instead, the chapter 'Decentred nations' analyses the ways in which the contradictions between the nation-state and global economic and cultural processes, like transnational corporations and television, work to decentre the nation from without, while simultaneously contributing towards the identifications, from within the nation, of cultural and economic diversity and their expression in national identities and notions of the national interest against the power of global corporations and media moguls.

The argument of this chapter is that the critics who have suggested we are now in the era of postnationalism need to re-examine the ways in which they have arrived at this conclusion. It is based on the idea that either there are nations or there is globalisation which ruptures the national project. However, this is seen to be a very superficial view of the ways in which nations are constituted in the first place. Instead, it can be demonstrated that nations are constituted in multi-centric ways which means that they are not unitary and that they hold within them a vast array of both centring and decentring mechanisms.

Thus, nation-states in Latin America have been produced as much from diversity as the power of the homogenising national narrative. The military has played an important role in the calling into being of a unitary nation linking national subjects to specific territory but even this is not as settled as it would seem to be. In the case of Ecuador the boundaries of the nation are one major area of contestation. Borders mark the nation but so, too, does a sense of national identity and the national is an ideologically constructed space bounded by legally enforceable rules. However, difference and the diasporas that have over the centuries made the nation-states of Latin America are another means by which the nation is decentred and disassembled, provoking a rupture within the 'fictive ethnicity' around which the national is imagined.

In the second part of the book we continue to explore the theme of rupture in the 'Migration and globalisation' chapter. We begin by questioning the current orthodoxy which tells us that we live in a world where the process of globalisation has reached a point where national boundaries, economies and cultures are of little importance. We do not deny the significance of the activity and investment decisions of transnational capital nor the revolution in communication technologies that have transformed the ordering of time and space in our lives. Do we live in a postnational global cultural economy? We share Michael Smith's scepticism on this view. Smith argues against the view on several counts, not only pointing to the way in which affluent countries have introduced increasingly restrictive immigration policies (policies we should add which are never gender neutral) but also:

> Paradoxically, the expansion of transnational migration has re-sulted in outbursts of entrenched, essentialist nationalism in both sending and receiving locales. In receiving cities and states, movements aimed at recuperating and reifying a mythical national identity are expanding as a way to eliminate the penetration of alien 'others'. States of origin on the other hand are re-essentialising their national identity and extending it to their nationals abroad as a way to maintain their loyalty and flow of resources 'back home'.
>
> (Smith, 1999: 11)

The symbolic construction of the 'other' and its demonisation is not just a feature of contemporary nationalist discourses but has been a discursive feature of nation-state building over time in an effort to drag populations away from local, at best regional, identifications to socially and politically constructed national identities. Thus, from Spain's expulsion of Moors and Jews in the fifteenth century to the calls of Jean Marie le Pen of the *Front National* for an end to the 'Islamification' of France in the 1990s or the election of Haider's Freedom Party in Austria at the beginning of the new millennium, the process is remarkably enduring.

But this chapter also wants to point to the ruptures in theory that have occurred over time. These 'ruptures' or theoretical 'breaks' have not always moved us forward in the theorisation of migratory processes, quite the reverse, they often resulted in a theoretical impasse. To reiterate, on the one hand there were the economistic accounts of labour migration in the 1950s and 1960s, characterised by an emphasis on the rational calculations of individuals or households. On the other hand there were the neo-Marxist interpretations in the 1970s and early 1980s of the same phenomenon. Somewhere in between the metaphorical 'baby' got thrown out with the bath water. It seemed that linking structure and agency had become too problematic and was shunted into the 'too difficult tray'. Attention refocused on the institutions in between the two (see Boyd, 1989). Households and social networks became the focus of much research. While not denying the importance of households in being a motivator for migration, as we shall see they are quite central to the decision to migrate, they and the social networks of migrants and would-be migrants cannot provide a full picture of the means through which contemporary migrant labour 'systems' operate. As Goss and Lindquist argue:

> the employer and the complex networks of recruitment agencies that link it with the migrant are remarkable in their absence in most accounts of international labour migration.
>
> (1995: 337)

The institutionalisation of both legal and clandestine migration as a 'business', particularly in Asia, is often overlooked, yet there is evidence to suggest that this role may be crucial in facilitating new flows (Hugo, 1994). Even asylum seekers may resort to this method of flight. The formation of social networks which facilitate migration for others may then only be a secondary development.

Goss and Lindquist (1995) and Richmond (1988) have used Giddens' structuration thesis in their attempts to provide a more grounded sociological theory of migration and we use Richmond's model to examine the flow of ethnic Russians back into the 'motherland' after the break-up of the Soviet Union.

We go on to consider whether the current preoccupation with 'transnationalism' does in fact constitute another theoretical rupture. One of the problems with the term is that it is used in a number of different ways. Does it include the simple act of remittance sending by first generation migrants to the family at home as well as the Chinese 'astronauts', described by Portes, who live in the US and commute across the Pacific to do business (Portes, 1997)? Portes argues that transnational communities are

> dense networks across political borders created by immigrants in their quest for economic advancement and social recognition. Through these networks, an increasing number of people are able to lead dual lives. Participants are often bilingual, move easily between different cultures, frequently maintain homes in two countries, and pursue economic, political and cultural interests that require their presence in both.
>
> (Portes, 1997: 812)

This would seem to rule out our first generation remittance senders, particularly those whose position in the destination country is legally insecure. Moving easily between two cultures may only be a dream, but one that is worth fighting for by the millions of men and women across the globe whose presence in the migration setting is either insecure or, worse, rendered 'illegal' by immigration policy.

But such people do occupy transnational social spaces, often having moved on from place to place but always retaining their links with their 'homeland' and forging new social networks with compatriots in the migration setting. Given the lack of conceptual clarity over the term it is difficult to say whether there is anything new going on here. For instance, Indian trading minorities have occupied transnational social spaces since the thirteenth century. The development of air travel and mobile phones may have made their business life easier but these facets of contemporary life cannot explain their existence.

The politics of belonging

In a collection called *Locality and Belonging*, the editor, Nadia Lovell, argues:

> Yet belonging, with all its pragmatic connotations and potential for tying people to place and social relationships, also evokes emotions, sentiments of longing to be in a particular location, be it real or fictive.
>
> (Lovell, 1999: 1)

This has a special resonance for our explorations of the politics of belonging in which we consider the ways in which both the nation and migration form loci of sentiments and emotions crucial to a sense of home.

In both parts of the book we explore the politics of belonging. In Part I Sallie Westwood explores the ways in which a sense of belonging is forged in relation to national identities and the investments that are made in these constructions, suggesting that there are specific moments, or sites, in which the subjective experience of being a member of a nation comes together with specific national events very often related to forms of popular culture. 'Political love', suggests Anderson (1991), is one way in which nationness is expressed and while his writing concentrates upon the literary canon produced in the name of patriotism, this chapter suggests an alternative route for understanding the sense of belonging produced through national identities. By focusing attention upon popular culture the analysis suggests that belonging is not fixed despite the level of ideological investments made by the nation-state. Instead the sense of being a part of the nation is contingent upon specific moments which tie individual biography and national history together. The most recent and developed popular cultural form is football, globalised and yet nationalised through the medium of the television which allows for a space in which individual subjectivities can share some part of the wider national preoccupation. This coming together is better conceptualised, suggests Sallie Westwood, as a 'correlative imaginary'. The terminology suggests connections within the spaces of the nation without the attendant difficulties of the notion of 'political love' which commentators have seen as corrupted by the excesses of nationalism displayed in war, aggression, racism and ultimately genocide.

Belonging to the nation places people in the world but for many this is a world on the move, a transnational world with ever-increasing levels of migration and settlement in places beyond the borders. The following chapter, 'Imagining America', seeks ways in which to examine the Latin American diaspora in the US and the ways in which the Americas are bound to one another over time. How is a sense of belonging and home forged within this wider conception of America? The US is increasingly a bilingual nation in which in some of the major cities it is more usual to hear Spanish on the streets than English. But this has not always been accepted and has produced a fierce backlash against Latino/a cultures.

Nevertheless, the 'Latinisation' of the US continues apace. This is to be found especially in popular cultural forms that are generated and sustained in the lives of diasporic populations in the city, creating new identities and a sense of belonging within specific urban spaces. There are those too who still occupy spaces at the margins, forging lives within rural employment and bringing the skills of barrio organisations and land invasions to the Texas landscape; again, seeking to make a home within what has often been a hostile environment that seeks persistently to remind the new migrants that home is elsewhere and cannot be imagined within the US.

In Part II of the book we explore these politics of belonging in a different way. In 'Sex work, domestic work: transnational household strategies' we look critically at the way in which the household has been conceptualised in migration theory and reconsider its meaning and its role for those women who have left 'home' to become transnational migrants. Half of all migrants in the world today are women, often working in harrowing and hazardous conditions in an effort to send money 'home' in the form of remittances and make a better life for themselves. But migrant women have even fewer options for employment than they had twenty years ago and restrictive immigration policies relegate many to clandestine work. Sex work and domestic work are often the only forms of work available, yet each represents the commodification of highly personal and emotional relationships. Nor is it a coincidence that so often it is migrant women who are recruited to these jobs. Just as the migrant domestic workers may be preferred by an employer precisely because she is the 'other' and can be treated with less respect, so is the sex worker. Kamala Kempadoo argues that the exoticisation of the third world 'other' is as important as economic factors in positioning women in sex work (Kempadoo, 1998: 10). Workers in both industries are rendered highly vulnerable by their racialised and gendered positioning in countries where they have no citizenship rights and, for many, no employment rights either, yet the empirical data that we refer to in this chapter bear testimony to the courage and resilience that they demonstrate in their personal and collective transformatory projects. In this chapter we hear from one group of migrant domestic workers in Britain who are undergoing the process of regularising their immigration status. All of the women concerned had entered the country under a concession that basically institutionalised the fact that they 'belonged' to their employer. If they left the employment of their named employer, they could not legally work for anyone else and when their original visa expired their right to remain in Britain disappeared. The concession was widely abused by employers and a broad-based campaign with domestic workers at its heart worked to change the concession and regularise the immigration status of those women who had run away and become overstayers due to no fault of their own. Thus the politics of belonging in this case is a straightforward struggle for justice in the migration setting which for some has become 'home'. Interviews with women undergoing the process of regularisation point to the importance of how a sense of belonging shifts over time and space, while virtually all still manage to send money to households at 'home', for those who have had children in London or those who left failing marriages, 'home' is now London but without 'papers' they cannot feel a secure sense of belonging.

Finally we turn to a consideration of what we term economic ethnoscapes and the role of transnational communities within them.

Economic ethnoscapes

In the final chapter of Part I of the book we return to the theme of globalisation in 'Diamonds are forever' and the way in which the selling and processing of diamonds in India has became a major growth area in the last two decades of the twentieth century. This is, however, also a story that has powerful gendered and ethnic components with a specific ethnic/religious group, the Jains, at the apex of the diamond trade. This chapter examines the narratives that comprise entrepreneurial stories with their emphasis upon risk and trust. But these components of the diamond trade are also stories of masculine values and they contribute to conceptions of masculinity within the Jain community. The ethnicisation of the diamond trade world-wide is familiar through the more well-known involvement of members of the Jewish communities in the trade. The Jains, however, are well known as gem traders and for their involvement in banking and commerce. In emphasising trust relations within the diamond trade many of the diamanteurs returned to the importance of kinship as the basic fabric of success in the trade and the ways in which familial relations are used strategically in business relations but also as a mode of surveillance against bad practice. Diamonds are not sold as simple ornaments but are marketed within a discourse of heterosexual love in which the diamond comes to stand for emotion and heterosexual desire. At the same time diamonds are attributed with endurance through the quality of the gem as a signal to the longevity of the relationship. This is powerful advertising and has been successful in increasing the sales of diamonds, especially in North America, where the bulk of the Indian trade is based. But diamonds have also to be cut and polished and the majority of cutters and polishers are in India working in a great variety of contexts from modern factories to small households in villages. Thus, there is often a distance between the rhetoric of the advertising and the relations of production. Those workers who cut and polish the diamonds are predominantly Gujaratis but they are not Jains. Latterly, some of those who started work as operatives have moved into trading but the trade remains stratified with the Jains at the top running the major companies who have also diversified into the production of jewellery in-house while they have moved into private medicine, airlines, the stock exchange, property development and so on beyond the trade, creating large companies in which familial relations are central.

These concerns are picked up in the final chapter of Part II of the book which explores the role of entrepreneurship among diasporic men and women and endeavours to 'de-essentialise' the notion of 'ethnic business'. In 'Men, women and business' we use two case studies; the first explores how largely South Asian entrepreneurs have reinvigorated an ailing British clothing industry and the second is a comparative study of service sector enterprises, to question 'cultural-ist' explanations for the rise in entrepreneurship amongst diasporic communities. Yet in enterprise the gendered division of labour persists, men are entrepreneurs and women, however central their role is to the viability of the business, remain in the shadows, their contribution often unacknowledged. In the British case this has produced some success stories for the owners of small businesses who in the nineties have increased the scale of their businesses and contributed to the rising power of a South Asian middle class, as well as those who moved into the 'seriously rich' list.

Conclusion

People are on the move, crossing borders and living in increasingly diasporic cities. This mobility is not, however, uniform and this book examines migration as mobilities of both the rich and the poor and the ways in which these two worlds come together. Crossing borders has profound effects upon individuals but also upon the ways in which national affiliations and the nation-state are understood. Globalisation is organised by capital but certain forms of trade, like the diamond trade, have been global since the trade began in the era of mercantil-ism. Equally, the trade in people has a long and undistinguished history which was globalised through enslavement. What does this mean now? In part this question is answered in the final chapters of this book where Annie Phizacklea examines the diversity which contemporary migrations represent and the differing diasporic experiences that they give rise to. This suggests that in constructing the transnational as a field of enquiry more attention needs to focus on the very different and unequal ways in which people experience transnationality as a major feature of globalising forces. Romanian gypsies fleeing the most recent chapter in a long history of persecution need to be as much a part of the story as the 'rich list'. Doreen Massey distinguishes between the jet-setters 'in charge' of initiating global flows and movement and those who are not in control of what is going on at all, the burgeoning number of refugees, asylum seekers and undocumented migrants: 'Here the experience of movement, and indeed of a confusing plurality of cultures, is very different' (Massey, 1993: 61). While we are supportive of this view we are equally concerned in this book not to deny agency to these seemingly 'powerless' players on the global stage who endeavour to manoeuvre, negotiate and wrest back economic, legal and cultural spaces of control and justice for themselves in their efforts to bring a better life to themselves and their families. At a subjective level, this may mean carrying bits and pieces of national identity around the globe, for instance the celebration of national days 'at home', supporting the national football team or through music, food and dance. But it means a good deal more than this. The vibrant hybrid cultures that this transnationalism brings with it may be celebrated but the stark realities of global city life are never far from the surface. Whether it be the civil rights campaign to end police brutality in New York (*Observer*, 26 March 2000: 23) or the campaign for justice amongst migrant domestic workers in London that we look at in the second part of the book, each example bears testimony to the individual and collective agency demonstrated by seemingly 'powerless' players on the global stage.

Part I

Chapter 1

Ruptures

Decentred nations: transnationalism and the nation in Latin America

Sallie Westwood

> The reality is quite plain: the 'end of the era of nationalism', so long
> prophesied, is not remotely in sight. Indeed, nation-ness is the most
> universally legitimate value in the political life of our time.
>
> (Anderson, 1991: 3)

Introduction

As Anderson suggests the saliency of nation-ness is not diminished and
yet the understandings of nations in a globalised world have shifted.
There is, indeed, a rupture in the ways in which we seek to analyse and
conceptualise nations and this chapter examines the move away from a
binary understanding of nations and globalisation to one in which the
complexity of these two processes is foregrounded. In part, this enters
a much older debate between those like Hobsbawm (1990) who
suggested the days of nation-building belonged to the late nineteenth
and early twentieth century and those like Anthony Smith (1991) who
is much more militant about the longevity of nations. In the British
case, following devolution, there has been an outpouring of commen-
tary on what Nairn initially called 'the break-up of Britain' and in his
more recent book calls 'after Britain'. More dramatically, Andrew
Marr entitles his book *The Day Britain Died*. For both old Britain is
disassembled. Nairn (2000) insists that Scottish independence is close
at hand while Marr (2000) suggests a new federalism, a reassembled
nation, that will constitute Britain for the twenty-first century. These
books, with their British focus, represent one part of an ongoing debate
about the political ruptures that constitute the new Europe. The

changes within nation-states in which the unifying national story has been disrupted are familiar throughout the world and demonstrate the importance of understanding that, while the forces of globalisation are powerful in reorganising national imaginaries, dissent and disruption from within the boundaries of nation-states are also part of the narrative. While the processes of decentring are all too evident in Britain, on another continent the externalities of the dollar economy have simultaneously further integrated the small nation-state of Ecuador while opening up a space for the politics of difference to challenge the hegemony of the national story. This challenge calls up a transnational politics specifically invoking the global fortunes of the indigenous peoples and practically forging political ties between indigenous groups and peoples in Ecuador and Bolivia. This chapter examines these processes as a way of undermining the binaries in which changing nation-states are too often understood, for example nation/globalisation and territory/territorialisations, the space of nations and the ways in which place and landscape are invoked in relation to a sense of belonging.

As the twentieth century disappeared one of the smallest nations, Ecuador, burst into the headlines when a coup overthrew the government and ousted the president, Jamil Mahuad, on 22 January. But this was no ordinary coup. It was the product of an alliance between the military and the indigenous organisation CONAIE (Confederation of Indigenous Nationalities of Ecuador) which had orchestrated street demonstrations and protests. The third player in this scenario was the US and the dollar economy which had arrived in Ecuador two weeks previously, wiping out savings and increasing the immiseration of an already impoverished population. The US brokered a return to civilian rule and the installation of a new president, Gustavo Noboa, the fourth president in two years, who immediately endorsed the move from the national currency, the *sucre*, to the dollar. The leader of the indigenous organisation, Antonio Vargas, has suggested that the new president has six months in which to address the problems of the nation (*Guardian*, 27 January 2000). This scenario, with the US directly involved in the affairs of Latin American nation-states, has a long history but it should not be read simply as a rerun of earlier decades when the US tried by every means to exercise military and political hegemony in Latin America. This is a moment in which the economic, political and cultural facets of globalisation are intertwined in novel ways. One of those ways is the growing power of the indigenous organisation, CONAIE, now a transnational organisation complete with website and an agenda which has brought an alliance with the military in Ecuador. This is part of a history of organisation by CONAIE in relation to the state in Ecuador in which the politics of difference has been foregrounded.

In 1996 Luis Macas, then president of CONAIE, was elected to the National Congress as a deputy and he suggested that this was a break with past politics and that it brought a new era of popular democracy in which the grassroots would now be represented in government. It was an important victory and brought social movement politics into the constitutional frame but it was not long before the social movements were back on the streets.

There were street demonstrations in February 1997 in which one man, a student, was killed, a general strike, claims and counter-claims to the presidency and a watchful military. Ecuadoreans in the capital especially were brought onto the streets by the depth of popular feeling in relation to the self-styled president '*el loco*', Abdalá Bucaram, and his neo-liberal economic policies. But, more than the substantive issues, the size of public demonstrations was a visual reminder of the strength of democratic culture in Ecuador and the willingness of citizens to take to the streets and protest. Equally, the tear gas and watercannon showed the power of the state and the availability of forces against popular protest. At one point Ecuador had three presidents – Bucaram who refused to go despite the congress passing a motion that due to mental instability he was unfit to be president, the deputy, Rosalia Arteaga, who did succeed Bucaram briefly, and the recent president Fabian Alarcón, supported by the military and the final outcome of the in-fighting. Fabian Alarcón was replaced electorally by Dr Mahuad, previously mayor of Quito, the capital city, in August 1998. In April 1997 the military filed a case for treason against Bucaram which he countered from exile in Venezuela, blaming the military for his summary dismissal. Overall, the ongoing and deepening crises in Ecuador demonstrate both the success of the national project and the contradictory play of decentring forces which destabilise the national project.

The national project in Ecuador has a long history but in the Bucaram era it was basically hijacked by the latest version of a parody of the 'populist despot' in the shape of the all-singing Bucaram, otherwise known as '*el loco*', who apparently delights in the name. He is a 'gesture politician' who previously fled Ecuador following corruption charges but who has powerful and wealthy friends in Guayaquil (the booming coastal city) and who mounted a populist media campaign in order to secure the presidency. As he has now been made aware both *el pueblo* and the media are uncertain friends. Politically Bucaram follows in the wake of other 'colourful' figures in Ecuador's history – *el Bombito*, for example, General Lara who was also fond of staging media events for his own self-aggrandisement. Bucaram is not entirely new in this and in many other ways as well. In terms of policy, if the incoherent twists and turns of his proclamations can be dignified in this way, his political rhetoric reinforces the earlier and current version of economic liberalisation which marks nation-states throughout Latin America and countries across the world. The two pillars of this are privatisation and structural adjustment which we know from the many studies of both make some folk rich and a lot of people a lot poorer. The recent events in the aftermath of 'dollarisation' demonstrate the ineffectiveness of these policies.

Nation/globalisation

In part, Ecuador, a specific nation-formation, shares with many others around the world a series of processes which both centre and decentre the nation simultaneously and it is these processes that are discussed in this chapter. It is especially interesting, both in relation to Latin America more generally and in relation to Ecuador, because Ecuador is a small country overshadowed, in many respects, by her larger neighbours, Colombia, Peru, and Venezuela – all also in the news for the complex economic and political processes that mark the current conjuncture. Ecuador is a nation-state of some ten million people (1991 census) with both defined and contested borders, the latter crucial to the nation-building project in the country.

From its split with Grand Colombia in 1830 to the present day Ecuador has been engaged on a nation-building project that is both successful and contested. Since its inception there has been a major contestation between the three distinct regions, the Costa, the South and the highlands, which continues today and is exacerbated by the counter processes of globalisation. The coming together of these three regions into a state taking its name from the Equatorial line brought together a sense of territory with the development of the state and conceptions of Ecuadorean nation-ness from the late nineteenth century (Quintero-Lopez, 1987; Clark, 1994). These official forms of nation-building are the classic period of Anderson's analysis, the Liberal revolution, from which infrastructural developments were generated, schooling was envisioned, the national money the *sucre* was inaugurated and state structures around law and order, taxation and citizenship emerged. Central to the nation-building project throughout has been the military which, as in other states, defined issues of national security but within a situation where, over time, the military organised productive capacity through factories making all kinds of things from foodstuffs to military boots, a bank and latterly the organisation of a football team under the name *Nacional*. The military vision of Ecuador has also changed over time (Isaacs, 1993). But key moments were the 1960s and 1970s when the military embarked upon a self-conscious modernising and populist integration programme in which the African and indigenous descent populations were to be integrated through community development, technical schools and drafted into the army for military service – although many of the respondents in a recent study (Radcliffe and Westwood, 1996) had avoided this by one means or another. This was a marked shift in the imaginary of the nation which had previously placed these sections of the population at the periphery of the nation in relation to an ideology of *mestizaje*. Instead, this new inclusivity was located in a vision of the nation with a refashioned history and national time/space frame. For those who were the recipients of these policies it looked rather different and was characterised as colonial incursions, a language still in use by peoples in Amazonia and the highlands. This was a changing nation-building project generated from within but also from without. Ecuador has always been produced as a national entity against the externalities of both North America and, closer to home, Peru, which is the 'enemy on the border'. This is a border which still erupts into periodic wars (most recently 1995; see Radcliffe, 1996), confrontations and stand-offs (most recently 1997), and peace treaties (most recently 1999) which is constructed as the national line which must be defended at all costs in the interests, not simply of national security, but national integrity. Put simply, Peru is 'the Other' of Ecuadorean national identity. It is the centring mechanism, called up by government, politicians and most importantly the military.

Against this centring, from the beginnings of national projects, has been the attendant and increasingly contradictory process of globalisation. Raymond Williams (1983), for example, saw no contradiction because nation-states were an efficient way to organise orderly markets for the global development of capitalism. This economistic account ignores, of course, the huge emotional, cultural and ideological investments on the part of states and individuals in the nation-building project. All of these processes are part of the globalisation process as much as the economic relations which tend to be privileged in extant accounts of the globalising power of finance capital. Nevertheless, in complex and subtle ways the current processes of globalisation are ostensibly marked by a lack of contradictions glossed in an account of niche marketing of places and peoples in relation to the consumption of the world through tourism. One of the major ways in which the global and the local are brought together is through the selling of folkloric elements, including ethnicities, as part of the tourist package, from postcards to the workers in the major hotels. Crain's (1996) account of the ways in which hotels recruit women workers in Quito on the basis of their ethnicity, which is reinvented for tourist consumption and performed in relation to a specific market, is one example of the negotiations between nationals and the economic demands of global consumption. The women involved are not unknowingly inserted into the tourist trade but are conscious of the aesthetics of tourism and they maximise their difference in the sale of their labour power. Equally well known are the traders of Otavalo in Ecuador with their distinctive dress and folk idiom which is marketised around the world, especially to North America, where they sell their now famous woven wall hangings. Kyle (1999: 437) in a study tracing the historical roots of this transnational trade emphasises recent changes to production and the use of materials and the ways in which traders 'jealously guard client contacts' in an increasingly globalised market. The clothes that the Otavalan traders wear and the long plaits of the men enhance the notion of authenticity just as the dress and demeanour of the women working in the hotels do.

However, to emphasise the global versus the local as though it were a new phenomenon is also problematic, for what Williams and countless others remind us is that the global was ever-present and that most modern states were in part generated out of plunder, colonial expansion and a protest against both. The historical global processes included both centring and decentring elements throughout – the African disapora and enslavement which moved African peoples around the globe, the plantation economies, the trade in goods, and the development of economies in relation to the unequal exchange of capitalist development are in part a shared history.

This history of unequal exchange and exploitation of peoples, products and land which has generated capitalist development also produced what was called a 'comprador bourgeoisie' with interests allied to Western capitalism rather than indigenous concerns in the home country. But this was always only one part of the story. It did not give enough credibility to indigenous development and the power of indigenous capitalism (this has been noteworthy in accounts of India, for example). However, the importation into Latin America (encouraged by the US) of neo-liberal economic programmes has put a new spin on the relations between nations and global economic processes. The interesting contradiction in these processes is that while transnational corporations, like the oil companies Texaco and BP in Ecuador and Colombia, decentre the nation, they also provide a focus for national feeling and a way of mobilising national sentiment – as President Bucaram discovered, like politicians before him. In 1993–4 in Ecuador there were large street demonstrations against the privatisation programmes, especially the privatisation of electricity. Central to the protest and alongside the labour unions and citizens was the army who protested against the sell-off on the grounds of national security. This is because more than at any previous juncture privatisation means foreign capital can buy up what have previously been seen to constitute national assets – electricity, water, telecommunications, coal, minerals, etc. (as can be seen in the case of the Philippines, for example, which is now all but owned by multinational corporations with US parent companies). The subtle version invokes a partnership with national government or local capital – like the De Beers mines in

Namibia and Botswana where De Beers, the diamond cartel, owns half of the major national asset of these countries. The same processes have marked the 1980s and 1990s in Latin America and a small country like Ecuador burdened by debt was easy to sell. Inevitably, the privatisation programme was coupled with a World Bank structural adjustment programme culminating in Ecuador becoming a dollar zone. National governments then become management committees for a model of capitalist development which involves an endless round of negotiations with multinational and large corporations and the World Bank – out of which are claimed the great success stories like Chile. The media coverage suggests success. The *Guardian* (15 February 1996), for example, ran the headline 'Dancing to a happier beat in Latin America' which celebrated the fall in inflation, the growth of consumption especially in Argentina, and the prospects for British investment overall, reminding business at a seminar in London that the British have a long history of investment in Latin America. However, fortunes have changed again and by now economic crises have made investors nervous once again. Chile remains favoured and successful, so much so that it is now planning to join NAFTA rather than the Latin American 'common market', MERCOSUR!

These globalisation processes have generated additional stories, including the attempt through international law to bring General Pinochet to trial for crimes against humanity following the overthrow of Allende in Chile. The long and protracted legal process succeeded in keeping the general in Britain for an extended period of time. Although he was returned to Chile on medical grounds and appears to be rather more healthy than was suggested, the process does signal the importance of a global public culture which seeks legal remedies. The attempt to make a head of state accountable in international law is also viewed as an affront to the integrity of the nation-state and contributes to the decentring of the nation.

However, the opposition to General Pinochet is not the only form of opposition. The guerrillas in Colombia regularly blow up the BP pipeline as part of an ongoing war of attrition and organised labour and allies have regularly protested against neo-liberal policies in Ecuador. In part, opposition groups can also learn from the processes of globalisation because multi-media televisual globalisation is not simply a homogenous product. Television is not a simple case of cultural imperialism as it was understood in the 1970s. This took no account of the differential receptions generated, in part, from the viewers in what Martin-Barbero (1993) has called 'mediations' — the encounter between the life experience and cognitive maps of the viewer with media products. Clearly, the US and latterly Rupert Murdoch do exercise an unprecedented level of control over media companies but this does not automatically translate into specific products. (*Sun* journalists in Britain occupy a variety of ideological positions, some deeply opposed to the *Sun* — a tabloid newspaper owned by Murdoch.) Equally, the fourth largest media company in the world is the Brazilian Globo company which exports media products including Xusha and *telenovelas* around the world (Simpson, 1993). Importantly, for the politics of protest and contestation, street demonstrations are good television and protests in many parts of the world are globalised, whether it is workers in the streets of Quito or in Taiwan, or eco-warriors protesting against genetically modified foods or against the World Trade Organisation. Many groups learn lessons and tactics from this global news constructed by CNN or BBC WorldWide as the purveyors of images and text. As many of the media studies have shown it is not possible to simply read a message from the political economy of media ownership, but there are frames in which representations are produced. For example, 'making the news' does rely on being in places already designated newsworthy with the relevant technology to hand. The diversity of media companies via satellite means, however, that these companies are available for news coverage as the Zapatistas have shown, especially in tandem with the use of the World Wide Web.

While the global media make world citizens of us all, including people in Ecuador and Colombia, these countries also have their own networks and the promotion of a national story through television and programming — the nine o'clock news is a familiar story of national time in countries around the world. This presents a vision of the nation to itself and politicians are keenly aware of the role of television in the making of the nation. For the most part national TV works within the frame of official nationalisms and contributes towards discourses that present the nation, its politics and concerns as well as its national identity in specific ways. But, and this is a very large but, these are always contested in terms of the ethnic composition of the presenters and viewers, the regional and class bias of the stories, etc. Against this is the global realm, and, especially for Latin America, North America, which offers a re-presented world through the media. This is not, however, a binary in which the North and the South are separated; they are constantly in forms of interplay and especially now through the movements of peoples from the South to the cities of the North. Viewers can consume the same products around the globe (music, news, sports) but this globalisation also becomes a mirror against which the local is seen and contributes to the world of differences of which nation-states and myriad national identities are a part. The recent statement from Cuba, for example, which insists that the US cannot decide which television networks it will set up in Cuba, only the Cuban government can do this, illustrates the point. However, satellite technology means that no government is quite in a position any more to control media products being beamed into nation-states (as India discovered – from one channel it now has 60 and more stacked up waiting to join in). What does happen is that global media products will be indigenised – *24 Hours* in Peru, for example. The proximity of nation-states in Latin America also means cross-border viewers. Although produced and anchored in Peru, the programme *24 Hours* is watched avidly by people in Colombia.

One of the ways in which many of these concerns come together is in the *telenovela* which often presents the story of the nation in relation to the human interest narrative of love, lust and betrayal. Some, like *Café*, produced in Colombia and now exported world-wide, clearly use a national sign – coffee. But, Ecuador has not produced a national soap but imports soaps (recently *Café*) often from Mexico produced by Mexican companies on location in Miami. These are hybrid products for an increasingly hybrid cultural realm (Canclini, 1995). The importance of *telenovelas*, as I have previously suggested, is that they generate a national space shared in time and place by viewers with a series of culturally transparent referents which can become a common currency and create a sense of belonging essential to the production of national identities explored more fully in the chapter that follows. Conversely, the fact that these are hybrid, imported cultural products can also destabilise the sense of the national and within the contradiction between the two effect a destabilisation of the national cultural space and a disassembling of the nation. As Bauman (1998: 2) notes, 'Globalization divides as much as it unites, it divides as it unites.'

Bauman's despairing account of globalisation is a counter to the optimistic, 'happy-clappy' version of the complex and multi-faceted processes that constitute globalisation. For Bauman we are either 'tourists' or 'vagabonds' divided between the spoils of space-time compression or victims of the global financial markets and trans–national corporations. These processes flatten cultures, turn subjects into consumers and places into holiday destinations as part of the inexorable McDonaldisation of the world. Intentionally polemical, Bauman takes broad sweeps at a phenomenon that is economic, political and cultural. It is also clear from the foregoing discussion that these processes should be periodised to account for the early adventurers, empire builders and the colonial consolidators. The chapters in this book suggest accounts of transnational processes that constantly shift the binary that is the basis of Bauman's account.

Territory/reterritorialisations

The power of the multinationals within nation-states, controlling major resources and what had been conceived of as national assets, from oil and minerals to power and telecommunications, coupled with the globalisation of the media and television, raises further contradictions for the issue of territory. Territory marks the space of the nation. It is integral to conceptions of nationhood and becomes a sign for the nation or one to strive for in the case of the dispossessed – the homeland, a potent symbol of the integrity of a people and the coming together of the people and the nation in place. Place has powerful resonances for national identities and offers people a cartography of belonging. It is woven into national stories through the remembrance of battles and the defence of space. In relation to Ecuador, this is regularly played out in relation to the Other of Ecuadorean nation-ness: Peru, the enemy on the border with whom Ecuador has an old dispute over territorial rights. Equally, landscape is offered as a familiar and shared experience for members of a nation and invested with powerful emotional and nostalgic portent within forms of official nationalisms (the English landscape is the classic example with its naturalisation devoid of class and racial markers). Ecuador takes its name from the Equator, is known for the volcanic mountain, Cotopaxi, with its snow cap and equally for the Galapagos islands. Latterly it is also marked by the heritage city, Quito. But the lived experience of locality very often proves to be more powerful. In part because the exclusions of location are classed, racialised and gendered and the national treasure of landscape and territory do not resonate with all equally. Instead, in Ecuador the majority of people of African descent identify with the coastal area, the city of Guayaquil and the history of Esmeraldas with its autonomy and celebration of difference through the power of the black population. Now there is an embryonic organisation, FCUNE. But these regional variations and loyalties which so powerfully decentre the nation are only one part of the decentring of territory. This contradiction is also played out in relation to the processes of globalisation which see markets not nations, assets not national resources (see the discussion in King, 1996, for example). However, given the postmodern turn and attention to niche marketing, nations and cultures can be recycled on the basis of their specificities in relation to global capitalism. Territory does bring into sharp relief the contradictions of the couplet nation-territory. In Ecuador, for example, there is a demonstrable willingness to go to war over land and borders drawn on a map while the recent privatisations ensure that foreign capital exercises a controlling interest in basic resources.

However, this does not go uncontested and part of the contestation is couched within discourses on the nation, national interests and national identities. In the 1994 protests against privatisation in Ecuador this was the key rhetoric and one which could bring diverse sections of the population, from the military to the trade unions, together in defence of the nation – the economic war which seeks to confirm the place of the nation in both a geographic and symbolic sense. In the protests over Bucaram (February 1997) the coalition adopted the title Patriotic Front, reclaiming the national from below. Bucaram shifted this designation and called the protests a 'civilian coup' – an interesting juxtaposition. In 2000 the same coalition was again brought onto the streets but with increased military support through the alliance between the indigenous organisations and the army. These contestations from within are part of a reframing which also has another agenda concentrated on a process of reclamation and is organised through CONAIE in the struggle for land. Land ownership is still concentrated in the hands of a few, although in 1994 CONAIE made major strides forward in the development of redistribution and the claims by indigenous peoples to land rights in Amazonia. The recently deposed president undermined this development. But, especially in Amazonia, the mapping exercises using local knowledge to physically stake out land and claims through the courts against Texaco via the work of an allied organisation OPIP have had some successes (Radcliffe and Westwood, 1996). These claims are located both in time and space with areas being marked out by local peoples who know and have lived the history of the land. These are local 'homelands' and a crucial economic resource for local people and part of the claims against the power and legitimacy of national governments to offer territory to oil companies for exploration and processing. Against the national these are local claims but, in another twist, these reterritorialisations are also part of a political agenda which looks beyond the nation and to the generation of a collectivity of indigenous peoples which is transnational and, through the global media, can call up transnational support as the indigenous peoples of the Brazilian rain forests have sought to do.

Imaginary/fictive ethnicities

The issues involved in the politics of place are not only economic relating to land as territory and its symbolic power in relation to the nation, the issue of who is part of the imaginary of the nation is crucial and relates to racisms and racialisations. Racisms are part of the complex which organises the imaginary of the nation producing homogeneity, organised through the state, which defines, through the legal/military complex, the borders of the nation, not only in terms of territory but also in terms of the geographies of exclusion that constitute citizens and aliens. These legal definitions are strongly allied with the imaginary of the nation and, as Mallon (1995) notes in relation to Mexico, certain sections of the population remain unimagined within the nation which leads to contestations at the symbolic and legal levels. In Ecuador this is one of the challenges from CONAIE who refuse the official version of the nation and its organisation around the ideology of *mestizaje* and racial democracy. The Latin American case is especially interesting because the imagined community of the nation is organised in relation to a fictive ethnicity which is hybrid – the *mestizo/a*. This fictive ethnicity is given legal power and enshrined in the constitution and the bureacratic procedures of the state – for example, the lack of ethnic data in the census in many Latin American countries and certainly in Ecuador.

The nation-state produces abstract legal notions of citizenship with rights and responsibilities on a liberal model of equality before the law and the right to vote. These notions are important and sustain a terrain of dissent which can call up the rhetoric of rights and distributive justice (Walzer, 1983) in the interests of specific groups. Claims to nationhood via these abstract forms, to the citizen and the 'fictive ethnicity' around which notions of national identity are formed, are crucial to the centring of the nation and discourses and practices are organised to sustain the fictions – through schooling, national days, celebrated heroes, flags, monuments – the whole panoply of cultural/symbolic artefacts that contribute towards the imaginary of the nation and are re-presented to the populace as the nation of which they are a part. (In 1994, for example, a popular Ecuadorean television programme, *La TV*, generated a series of discourses which reclaimed an Ecuadorean inidigenous past. The series was presented by Freddie Ehler who later went into politics and fought against Bucaram in the presidential elections of 1996.) These national stories are part of the way in which national identities are constructed as fictions represented by an ideal national who is ethnicised in a specific way. But what happens when the national becomes embodied – sexualised, gendered, ethnicised and racialised, all of which decentre and hollow out the notion of 'the national'?

It is precisely on this terrain that a politics of difference and identities is played out. Thus, the African Ecuadorean presence in Ecuador, the histories and present day lives of people of African descent, has to be part of a politics, made visible and placed in the nation. In a similar more vocal and organised way the CONAIE have placed this difference on the agenda and called for the constitution to acknowledge this in adopting a constitution of pluri-nations. It is interesting in itself that counter-hegemonic forces like CONAIE also privilege the terrain of the nation and this, in part, relates to the processes of racialisation. Racisms are regimes of power and they come to bear upon embodied subjects who are simultaneously individualised and objectified – i.e. individual subjects come to represent a racial category, to stand in for the 'race'. The claim for a recognised difference is one way to turn the visibility that is so crucial to racialisation, and the forms of racism in operation via disciplinary modes, on its head and to claim a self-defined visibility. This is not an easy task for CONAIE because they have both to define the terrain of a politics of difference while simultaneously generating a collective subject from the diversity of indigenous peoples in Ecuador. More recently the organisation has also generated a series of discourses on the issue of racism against people of African descent.

Racisms are not stable fixed entities and the discourses within which racisms operate twist and turn from, the still extant, biologically marked racist accounts to cultural racisms. Both were, and are, in operation in Ecuador where there is a tendency to use biological arguments and the body as biological signifier in relation to the population of African descent, on the racist assumption that the African descent population left their culture in Africa centuries earlier, to the cultural mode into which the indigenous peoples are inserted. Obviously, these are not exclusive categories – colour, physiognomy are used as markers of difference. But, they can be reappropriated as the 'Black is Beautiful' campaign demonstrated. The responses, too, are not singular and relations between different peoples are the product of ongoing negotiations. This produces and reproduces multiplicity and shifting imaginaries of the nation which are central to the lived experience of being Ecuadorean.

Official/popular/representation

These multiplicities, as I have suggested, can also use the rhetoric of the national – the claims against multinational corporations or the CONAIE constitutional reforms – in relation to a progressive and democratic vision of Ecuador. But it is important not to fall into the trap of viewing the binary official/popular as signalling authoritarian versus democratic or reactionary versus progressive. Popular forms of nationalism can certainly be progressive as the vision from CONAIE, or the earlier anti-colonialist struggles, or Cuban nationalism versus the USA. But there are forms of popular nationalism that are allied with the most reactionary politics and murderous racisms – like the British National Party in Britain, and the forms of masculinist racisms that leave young black men like Stephen Lawrence murdered at a bus stop in South London. Work by Cohen (1988), for example, emphasises the 'nationalism of the neighbourhood' in relation to white working-class men in Britain and locates the territorial imperative with locality rather than the imaginary of the nation and the boundaries of the nation-state. In the British context these often produce the most virulent racisms and 'geographies of exclusion' (Sibley, 1995) in the name of defence of space or territory. There can, however, be alternative versions of neighbourhood nationalism not tied to masculinist racisms but, rather, as we see in many of the urban barrios of Quito or Guayaquil and throughout Latin America, forms of resource politics organised by women addressing material needs in localities.

The politics of difference is not, of course, confined to issues of ethnicities but is importantly a gendered politics and a politics of sexualities, both of which are racialised and classed. National identities are organised around a heterosexual romance for the nation, the mothers and fathers of the nation, the sons and daughters and the familial rhetorics of the national story which give no place to homosexual and lesbian identities. Homosexual and lesbian identities, of course, decentre the imaginary of the nation to such an extent, it seems, that while there is a racialised politics in full view of the state, certainly in Ecuador the state has moved against homosexuality where it is an offence under the penal code. There is a very small and still underground queer politics in Ecuador and a more developed and open gay cultural politics in Colombia.

These issues raise the importance of overcoming the binaries within which much of our work is organised and which fuels much of the sexist, homophobic and racist politics for which nationalist discourses are infamous. Binaries work on fixity and fixed positions black/white, male/female, gay/straight and the notion of a unitary subject defined by a single identity. But the lived experience of blackness, whiteness, masculinity and so on belies this fixity. In all areas, whether it is a vision of the nation, of landscape and representations of the nation, there is fracturing and multiple readings and it is this complexity that is central to the theorisation of nations and national identities. How, otherwise, are we to understand the myriad ways in which the ideological work of sustaining a vision of the nation takes place?

Clearly, the official version of the nation sustains a constant process of assault from subaltern subjects but it is not either/or, as can be seen if we look at popular culture. Football, for example, is global, involving megabucks and is highly divisive and yet it can be raised to the status of bearer of the nation at the times of the World Cup or *Copa América* (Archetti, 1994; Mason, 1995). Soccer can be used politically both for and against repressive regimes and can generate local and national loyalties and vicious conflicts between rival supporters. National teams bear a heavy burden of national pride and expectation. Although Ecuador is not a major footballing nation, national pride is welded together with regional pride in the success of the Barcelona team from coastal Guayaquil.

Popular culture re-presents the nation to itself holding a mirror to 'the people' and televisual modes are crucially important in this work of representation. However, popular religion and popular forms of organising are also part of the terrain of representations. Most important in the Ecuador context has been the intervention by CONAIE in shifting the representation of 'the Other'. The political acumen with which the campaign for land, bilingual education and changes to the constitution has been waged and the way in which the government and military had responded prior to Bucaram put CONAIE at the centre of the politics of Ecuador. The struggles configured a new vision of Ecuador which held within it a reframed account of indigenous cultures and their presence in the nation-state. This is not confined to Ecuador but, as I have suggested, is trans–national, crossing boundaries and in this disassembling the vision of the nation and political borders. This, in part, brings us to the last theme of this chapter – state/civil society. CONAIE could organise from within civil society and take on the state in a mobilisation which has again occurred in relation to the Bucaram presidency.

State/civil society

Clearly, nations and states have grown up together but the full impact of nation-ness is generated and sustained in relation to the imaginary of the nation through civil society. In many Latin American states this is where conceptions of the nation were sustained in the call for a civil society against the military regimes of the 1970s and early 1980s. But, as before, there is no simple opposition between state and civil society. Analytically, in this chapter, the state is not understood voluntaristically as 'an actor' nor as unitary. Instead, the disassembling of the state and the multiplicities of sites that constitute the state generates an important politics from within state organisations and processes. This is especially relevant within the current phase of neo-liberal economic policies where, to use Gramsci's analysis, there are contestations in order to secure the state for a specific power bloc. Throughout Latin America there is the constant interplay between the military and a fractionalised bourgeoisie – fractionalised by region, ethnicities, sectoral interests. Consequently, the military in Ecuador did negotiate with CONAIE on land rights for indigenous peoples and bring landowners and the leaders of CONAIE together as part of a consensual, modernising ideology which was recently reinforced when the military negotiated within the ruptures of Ecuadorean politics. This is a complex politics and one that is in process. While across Latin America the military claims the legitimate use of force this is all but matched in Colombia, for example, by the counter claims of the guerrillas who are resisted by an ever-increasing share of the Colombian GNP and who contribute to the disassembling of the Colombian state.

Civil society too is a complex series of contestations with often fragile coalitions between trade union organisations, women's groups, ethnically based organisations, environmentalists, and so on. In Ecuador the main player in securing a form of collective subject of protest has been CONAIE, and the politics of land and indigenous rights has been privileged, which has had major repercussions for civil society and for all forms of political action struggling and negotiating for change at the state level. In addition, in Ecuador and Colombia, as in many of the Latin American states, the influence of liberation theology, 'worker-priests' and 'the option for the poor' has had an impact on organising and the rhetoric within which claims and demands are made which cannot be underestimated. Less influential to date, but increasingly important, is the role of the Protestant evangelist churches providing an alternative site for the play of powers within civil society. Inter-woven with the discourses generated and sustained in populist religion are those from television where 'the people' and the nation are also re-presented to citizens. Television, as I have suggested, can be a powerful tool in the generation of counter-hegemonic forces, raising issues in dramatic and very public ways and offering, as one channel in Ecuador did, forms of public accountability in which politicians were questioned and criticised for their actions in specific spheres. Several programmes were concerned with the oil companies and their impact on local people and the environment. One might also question the role of these forms of public shaming because they could be said to be managing protest through the media but in the Ecuadorean case the oil companies were already the subject of active and legal confrontations in Amazonia.

Conclusion

The preceding discussion has all too briefly foregrounded some of the contradictions between processes of centring and decentring in relation to the nation, specifically the nation-state formation of Ecuador in Latin America. In trying to analyse the twists and turns of nation and globalisation it is evident that the rupture in our under-standing is crucial to the theorisation of nations and nation-ness. In the reproduction of national narratives the importance of time and space as national time and space has been underlined. But these forms of national time/space are understood in relation to the power of the national organised around a fictive ethnicity which has been consis-tently challenged in the Ecuadorean case by the growing power of the indigenous organisation, CONAIE. Given the degree to which forces contribute to decentring and the fragmentation of nations and nation-states, it is all the more remarkable that subjects as citizens and nationals can claim and invest in a national identity. The fluidity within the official rhetoric of nations and states and the practices that contribute to the production of nationals is highly differentiated and complex. But it remains a powerful narrative which does speak to people and to which they have commitments, further explored in the next chapter. Recent research in Ecuador was conceived as a way of trying to understand this through a theorisation which sought to identify specific sites in which a sense of belonging and home is generated and sustained (Radcliffe and Westwood, 1996). The saliency of region, of place and ethnic identities provides nuanced encounters with the official versions of the nation and contribute to the pluri-nations that co-exist within the seemingly settled, or, in the case of Ecuador, not yet settled boundaries of the nation-state.

Notes

CONAIE – *Confederación de Nacionalidades Indigenas de Ecuador*; FCUNE – *Fundación para la Cultura Negra Ecuatoriana*.

Earlier versions of this chapter were presented at the universities of Amsterdam and Cambridge in 1996 and 1997.

Chapter 2

The politics of belonging

'Political love': popular culture and the national romance in Latin America

Sallie Westwood

> In an age when it is so common for progressive, cosmopolitan in-
> tellectuals (particularly in Europe?) to insist on the near-
> pathological character of nationalism, its roots in fear and hatred of
> the Other, and its affinities with racism, it is useful to remind our-
> selves that nations inspire love, and often profoundly self-sacrificing
> love.
>
> (Anderson, 1991: 141)

Introduction

The quote from Anderson with which I begin this chapter raises one of
the most important and enduring aspects of nations and national
identities – the powerful sentiments of national affiliations which
produce one moment in the politics of belonging. Anderson pursues
this in his elegant analysis but especially in relation to the ways in which
the nation is constructed in language as both 'the family' and 'home',
and it is these powerful invocations which are naturalised into a form of
'political love'. *La patria* invokes the motherland, redolent with notions
of family, home and a sense of belonging throughout Latin America.
Drawing on substantive work in Latin America, specifically Ecuador
and Colombia, this chapter concentrates upon the ideological work
that generates and sustains the powerful identifications of 'political
love'. However, this chapter offers an analysis which suggests that there
are specific moments and sites in which what I have called 'correlative
imaginaries', as an alternative to 'political love', are produced. Thus,
national sentiments are not a fixed attribute, a script that once learned
imbues the subject with a national identity and consciousness. Rather,

the national is a fragile coalescence called forth in specific time and space.

There is also a powerful critique of the attention to national sentiments, and its expression in patriotism, alluded to in Anderson's comments on 'cosmopolitan intellectuals' and the insistence on the negativity of a nationally based sense of belonging. Appadurai (1996), for example, expresses his concern in relation to the ways in which patriotism remains tainted by the racism of right-wing nationalisms and by the mode in which patriotism has been separated from the nation-state. Thus, he argues:

> But patriotism is an unstable sentiment, which thrives only at the level of the nation-state. Below that level it is easily supplanted by more intimate loyalties: above that level it gives way to empty slogans rarely backed by the will to sacrifice or kill.
>
> (1996: 160)

Appadurai's discussion is also prompted by the 'unselfconscious' ways in which there has developed a consensus around the notion that we are entering or living in postnational times. This requires much greater elaboration, suggests Appadurai, in an era when migration and diaspora have certainly tempered the ties of nations but seem in contradiction to have produced new discourses on homelands which are ethnically or religiously inscribed. The questions raised by Appadurai are central to the politics of belonging and his analysis suggests that the spaces between nations, those transnational spaces, are not yet spaces of belonging and do not come ready-made but are in the process of being created from the myriad diasporas and migrations that mark the modern world. Some part of this process is discussed in the next chapter 'Imagining America'. One of the problems relates directly to the language of transnationalism which, even without the hyphen, still speaks to a world of nations and boundaries on a binary model in which there is, or is not, the nation. Castells' (1997) model of flows tries to recast the argument in relation to the strategic role of nations within a developing global governance and the power of capital. Nations, though weakened, matter because without a national flag it is impossible to get into the game and negotiate with supranational organisations like the World Bank or the International Monetary Fund.

Nations/national identities

In theorising the nation and national identities I want to suggest that there are key sites in which these are produced. Very briefly, the first of these, following Anderson (1991), is the imaginary and the ways in which imagining nations provides the context in which national identities are called forth. The second site, articulated with the first, is the body as a site for the play of powers so crucial to the management, discipline and identification processes of nationalisms and national identities. But imaginary and embodied nations are lived through the discursive practices of everyday life elaborated in the popular with which I am primarily concerned in this chapter. Finally, the spatial, from the power of maps to symbolise the nation to the sense of place offered by localities, is another key site. These sites produce a series of articulations which both generate a fragile consensus – a centred nation – while simultaneously fracturing the nation, contributing to the decentring of the national. While this provides a framework within which it is possible to explore the saliency and variety of relationships to the nation and the complexities of national identities, it is also important to find ways of theorising the processes which interpellate subjects and explain the power of attachment, or, in another language, the investments made by subjects in their national identities. The term 'correlative imaginaries' is one attempt to provide a vocabulary for discussing the seductions of nation, nationalism and national identities. (This framework and an elaboration of 'correlative imaginaries' and 'geographies of identities', emphasising the saliency of place, are discussed in detail in Radcliffe and Westwood, 1996.)

The seductions of nationalism and national identities are, in part, an affair of the heart – what Anderson (1991) has called 'political love' – which for all its romance and emotion is still bound to the ideological work of nation-building. The term does, however, capture the huge emotional investments that people make in relation to their national identities, which states can call up in times of crisis and on which politicians lay claims. The concept, 'correlative imaginaries', is an alternative way of expressing this which is more consistent with an account of a decentred social and distinct from the fixity implied by the more spatial account of 'concentric circles of allegiance' (Williams and Smith, 1983). Correlative imaginaries generate and sustain an ideational horizontal integration within a shared space, through a form of interpellation which correlates subjectivities and social spaces. This allows individuals to place themselves within a 'frame' and to produce a form of identification between the self and the social, within specific sites. This placing – the generation of positionality – can, therefore, be said to be part of the ensemble of relations that produces national identities. Although there are many sites in which correlative imaginaries can be produced, this chapter concentrates upon their generation within forms of popular culture, especially televisual forms including football and *telenovelas* which have great emotional appeal.

The foregrounding of the popular is not intended to demote the importance of official discourses and practices in the construction of the imaginary of the nation and national identities. Nor is it intended to signal a binary, official/popular; both are ever present and form a constant mirror dance in which the ideological work of nation-building is conceived and executed in myriad ways across diverse sites. For some nations this encompasses a long historical trajectory in which institutional structures and official discourses have been designed in relation to nation-building to produce a 'national story'. One example of this process is to be found in the nation-state of Ecuador which is, of course, specific. But Ecuador shares with other states, both in Latin America and beyond, the task of generating a centred nation around a 'fictive ethnicity' bound to conceptions of hybridity and racial democracy through miscegenation. The latter has been clearly contested (Do Nascimento, 1989; Winant, 1992; Wade, 1993, 1997, for example) and found wanting – a myth located not with racial democracy but with a disavowal of blackness and an enhancement of whitening.

Ecuador: the national story

The beginnings of Ecuadorean national identity lie in independence from Gran Colombia in 1830. But the area that was to be Ecuador was, and still is, marked by strong regional identities represented by three cities, coastal Guayaquil, southern Cuenca and highland Quito, which became the capital city. All claimed the nation but an invasion by Peru in 1859 forced the three regions together in defence of the nation and began a process which remains unfinished in many ways. Only in the late nineteenth century did the administrative apparatus of a nation-state begin and the notion of a 'national interest' emerge. In 1885 the national currency, the *sucre*, was introduced and there were the beginnings of state education, military service and the development of an infrastructure of telegraph and railways. These forms of state organisation are consistent with Anderson's view of the 'official nationalism' that emerged in Europe during the same period.

Yet, the centralisation attendant upon the development of the state bureacracy did not secure the nation nor eradicate local and regional distinctions. Early on the Roman Catholic church had more impact in the sierra and less at the coast and education developed to match this with more secular schools at the coast. Increasingly, the imagining of the nation became secular, a consequence of the liberal view of the separation between church and state. Thus, civil marriage and divorce were introduced in 1902 and religious properties were nationalised in 1908.

While the imaginary of the nation was being formed within the tenets of the 'liberal' revolution this vision did not include those of indigenous and African descent who, as elsewhere in the Andean region, remained outside the nation but within the economic structures that sustained the imaginary of the nation. This did not go uncontested. Throughout the history of the region there have been revolts by those of African and indigenous descent and the early decades of the twentieth century heralded a new era of protest against the landowners and the development of disciplinary modes by the state in the form of the census, the role of the military and police appara-tuses. In 1942 the population of Ecuador was three million of whom it was suggested 39 per cent were indigenous and (in a confusion of categories well known throughout Latin America) peasant groups were 65 per cent with a literate population of 56 per cent (Quintero-Lopez and Silva, 1991: 313). During the 1950s and 1960s there were UN-sponsored programmes of national integration for the indigenous populations which were often characterised by these populations as colonial incursions.

Ecuador now has a population of over ten million (census 1991). Consistent with the celebration of hybridity in many other Latin American states, there are no statistics from the census on ethnicity. Ecuador is urban (55 per cent), literate (89 per cent), and a small state in which the centring of the nation and the saliency of national identities would appear to be attainable. Yet, Ecuador is a decentred nation fractured through racism and ethnicities, regional loyalties, class divisions, processes of globalisation and neo-liberal economic policies. The consistency of the centring project and official discourses on the nation are, in part, the product of the power of the military and the ongoing border dispute with Peru which erupts into small wars periodically. Peru is 'the Other' of Ecuadorean national identity and this notion of Peru as the enemy on the boundaries of the nation is powerfully sustained by military discourses on national security. But this is no simply repressive military machine but one committed to democratic processes, including human rights training and a modernising view of the role of the military as the only incorruptible force in Ecuadorean society.

The military plays a pivotal role in the national story of Ecuador, not only in terms of the claimed legitimate control over the means of violence but also through an inclusivist recruitment policy which is articulated in relation to indigenous and African-descent Ecuadoreans. The army also runs technical schools and community development projects in rural areas from the Andes to Oriente, an ideological school for the training of officers, a bank, a multiplicity of economic and industrial interests and, at the level of popular culture, it is the military that has the football team entitled *Nacional* and which includes most (over 50 per cent) black players. The influence of the military can also be seen in the national schooling system, based on a national curriculum which includes the history and geography of Ecuador and the region and the issue of national security in relation to Peru. Alongside this humanities curriculum is a social science civics course emphasising the duties of a patriot and the responsibilities of a citizen. All school books have the national anthem printed on the back cover and all children on transfer from primary to secondary school are inducted into the nation in a ritualistic and militaristic sense through a formal ceremony which involves swearing allegiance to the flag.

This curriculum is further reinforced as a national curriculum through the use of museums, monuments and knowledge of the founding fathers. One museum that all children visit is the *Mitad del Mundo* at the Equator line outside Quito. This is a small museum fashioned on the Guggenheim in New York, flanked by statues of the original French geodesic mission from the eighteenth century. Inside visitors are taken through a multicultural experience of Ecuador in which the diversity of Ecuador is foregrounded through exhibits which highlight forms of dress, work and, predictably for the African Ecuadorean population, forms of music and dance. It is a state-sponsored form of multiculturalism but it does attempt to be inclusive and the words that surround the museum emphasise this. Children enjoy the museum and take delight in the figures, the drums and, for many, the 'exotica' of Amazonia. This inclusivity and its emphasis upon difference co-exists with the complexities of an official account of Ecuador as both an Amazonian and an Andean country. The words *Pais Amazonica* are written under the shield that represents the nation. But the definition of the nation is bound to a fictive ethnicity which is hybrid, the *mestizo/a* and the ideology of *mestizaje*. In effect, this provides a racialised hierarchy in which whiteness correlates with high status, expressed by the *mestiza* Miss Ecuador who declared 'I am white'. This presence of 'whiteness' is underscored by the absence of 'blackness'. Ecuadoreans asked about the ethnic composition of Ecuador often enlarged the Andean and Amazonian indigenous population but, unless the respondent was a black Ecuadorean, rendered the black population of Ecuador invisible by omitting them from their account of the country. This tendency was less marked in the coastal city of Guayaquil and the province of Esmeraldas. Overall, however, the imaginary of the nation as a *Pais Amazonica* has become part of the national consciousness.

Despite the ideological work done everyday through schooling, the military, national celebrations, museums and the national hymn, racism, regional loyalties, ethnic diversities and the processes of globalisation constantly disassemble the national project in Ecuador and undermine the nation-building strategy. Thus, Ecuadoreans in Quito, historic capital of Ecuador, when asked for the meaning of *La Patria* responded by saying that it was a bus company (there is a bus company of this name which operates in Ecuador). This is interesting in relation to Maradona's comment, in a 1995 TV programme charting his life and times, that 'It is everyone's duty to be a patriot', confirming national sentiments despite his tortuous relationship with the Argentinian state in relation to football.

National space/time

One of the most important mediations between individual subjectivities and the imaginary of the nation is related to the ways in which national stories organise time and space. In so doing individual biography is framed by national events through official nationalisms which interpellate subjects as nationals. Nationals are called forth through the histories and geographies learned in school and celebrated in national days, ceremonies and events that mark the space of the national. The map of the nation-state is not simply inert territory with borders but a representational space into which biography can be inserted, offering a form of correlative imaginary which gives individual nationals a place in the national map. This produces, of course, a map of great diversity and complex variety against the homogenising nation-state account. Similarly, specific sites are offered as emblematic of the nation, in the case of Ecuador, the *Mitad del Mundo*, old Quito, the Galapagos islands, the mountain of Cotopaxi. However, when asked for a representation of the nation Ecuadoreans chose a huge variety of places and commodities like bananas or oil. The identification between national sentiment and land understood as territory and evocatively referred to as 'motherland' or 'fatherland' is very powerful in the production of political love, as Anderson (1991) suggests. But the story is made more complex because places do not exist in the national imagination as geographically inert. Instead, places, locations are racialised and suffused with the power relations of the nation-state. Consequently, areas of Ecuador, like coastal Esmeraldas, were commonsensically understood to be black and the black presence in the highlands or elsewhere was made invisible through forms of 'geographies of exclusion' (Sibley, 1995) which happen both through the social imagination and materially through the racist defence of space. Equally, land has a different political meaning within the discourses of the Confederation of Indigenous Nationalities of Ecuador (CONAIE) who, while promoting a pluri-nationalism, are united around the importance of land and against the incursions of military, government and the oil companies. Instead, indigenous peoples in Amazonia have engaged in their own mapping exercises and produced representations linked to their own histories and land rights.

Similarly, the official version of national time provides a history into which individual biographies can be inserted. Through the stories of the founding fathers, historic battles and ongoing wars, in this case related to the Ecuador/Peru dispute, individual biography is constructed as part of the history of the nation. This is reinforced and enacted through the national day and civic ceremonial alive with flags and emblems, all of which allows for correlations between individuals and the nation. This shared history, or national time, is represented in the monuments and museums in the major cities. These forms represent the nation to 'the people' and provide a performative nationism. While there is increasing attention to an indigenous past, resuscitated and revisioned, the African presence is a notable silence in this history and is not given a place in 'official' nation(al) time. The construction of national space/time is one part of the project of producing the imaginary of the nation, but, as I have already suggested, this is a fragile centring. Mallon (1995:18) characterises the production of nationalism as 'a series of competing discourses in constant formation and negotiation' and this is nowhere more evident than in relation to the role of the popular in the production of the national imaginary.

Popular space/time and correlative imaginaries

The distinction suggested by the binary official/popular is constantly undermined in the ideological work of nation-building. The official project of nationalism, like authoritarian populism, cannot succeed unless it generates a consensus with the active involvement of popular sectors. But this is itself a disassembled project relating to a number of sites which articulate both official and popular and interpellate subjects. One key moment in these processes is the mass media, most importantly television. Indeed, Rowe and Schelling (1991: 8) suggest that in relation to Latin America 'Modernity arrived with television rather than the Enlightenment', which may be an overstatement but it does highlight the importance of mass media forms in the Latin American context. Canclini (1995: 229), for example, notes, 'There was a method of associating the popular with the national that ... nourished the modernization of Latin American cultures.' The consumption of television especially is based upon an encounter, not a passive reception. Indeed, it can more specifically be characterised as an engagement or 'mediation' (Martin-Barbero, 1993) which itself generates and sustains differential receptions.

The interaction between the official and the popular can be clearly seen in the use of folkloric elements, for example, the representation of the nation through the figure of the indigenous woman or man so familiar in postcards and books for the tourist industry and the development of the trade in crafts and artefacts (Canclini, 1993). Equally, television has intervened very directly in the construction of the imaginary of Ecuador through a programme entitled *La TV* which has refashioned the history of Ecuador in relation to archeological finds which, it is claimed, are more spectacular than the pre-Columbian finds in Mexico. This claim to a specifically Ecuadorean heritage is framed by the nation-building strategies of state organisations like the Institute for Cultural Patrimony, keeper of all historic buildings and sites. This confirms Rowe and Schelling's view: 'it is probably valid to say that in Latin America the idea of folklore is bound up with the idea of national identity, and has been used by the state, among other things, in order to bring about national unity' (1991: 4). It is, of course, a familiar version of the reinvention of tradition known throughout the world. What is omitted from this are the mediations between the popular and the official expressed so clearly in the example used by de Certeau (1984: 31–2) in relation to Spanish colonisation of the indigenous peoples. He writes:

> the spectacular victory of Spanish colonization over the indigenous cultures was diverted from its intended aims by the use made of it ... the Indians [*sic*] often used the laws, practices and representations that were imposed on them by force or by fascinations to ends other than those of the conquerors. ... They metaphorized the dominant order; they made it function in another register.

This was, and is, most transparent in relation to Roman Catholicism, which has been popularised in spectacular ways throughout Latin America.

Conceptions of national space/time, as suggested above, produce a sense of correlation between individual biography and national histories and geographies but the attempt to create a sense of belonging requires an intervention of a more popular kind. In both senses the web of power which is constitutive of space/time is ever present (see Massey, 1995). Memory and acts of remembering within boundaries are vital elements productive of national identities and a sense of belonging. These productions are revisioned within popular cultures through festivals, television, songs and stories articulated with current politics to recast the political imaginary. Thus, the CONAIE organisation in Ecuador has reframed national time and conceptions of space within an alternative nationalism, a pluri-nationalism which is also a transcendence of specific national boundaries and an appeal to a transnational collectivity which transforms the space of national identities. CONAIE has successfully generated, from great diversity, a collective subject that can intervene in powerful ways in the political life of Ecuador demonstrated in the previous chapter. In part this is a product of the reframing of time and space which calls up a specific subaltern history in relation to place and land which transcends official histories of the nation.

This is one part of the multiplicity of stories that generate and sustain conceptions of the nation and destabilise the official project. Equally powerful is the ongoing story of American relations. In part it has been against the exterior of North America that the interior of the nation has been framed while the power of mass media forms, especially televisual worlds, has reframed conceptions of the nation in myriad ways, both centring and decentring the nation simultaneously. There is no simple form of cultural imperialism in operation but a series of mediations that have produced singers like Carlos Vives who combines rock styles with the rhythms of the Pacific coast and is an international export from Colombia.

Cultural imperialism understood as the export of US cultural products and values cannot account for the complexities of film and televisual products. There is no one-way traffic in the televisual medium. Globo television from Brazil is now the fourth largest television company in the world, home to the famous Xuxa (a very blonde talk-show presenter), now exported to the United States. More people in Brazil have televisions than have running water or refrigerators. Both Globo and the Mexican company Televisa export television programmes as cultural commodities throughout the world, including the blockbuster *telenovelas* for which Latin America is famous.

Telenovelas, watched by millions on a regular basis, have been the subject of considerable discussion, especially in relation to the gendering of popular culture and the radical/populist potential that is suggested by a genre which is narrative, easily read and polysemic (Martin-Barbero and Muñoz, 1992). In Ecuador, *telenovelas* imported from Mexico are prime time television, rivalled only by football for audience ratings and popularity. Based on romance, the *telenovela* is a powerful melodrama, building the stories of nations and states into the narratives of families complicated by numerous sub-plots. *Telenovelas* are, therefore, complex cultural productions, a carnivalesque form, suggests da Matta (1985:96), where 'the author, reader, and characters constantly change places'. These cultural products are also commodities with major corporate investments at stake.

The grand themes of *telenovelas* bring together families with the histories of nations and states, as in the recent *Café* in Colombia, now exported throughout Latin America, to the US and Europe. *Café* used all the classic conventions of *telenovela*: a wealthy family and the daughter of an alliance between a domestic and the son of the house. Their lives intertwined, generating a complex interplay of the personal and the social which made for riveting television watched by millions of viewers. Desire and sexuality were the key ingredients as the plot twisted and turned, representing the history of the nation through the characters, including an English man in the coffee trade. The issue of sexuality was foregrounded by the plot which hinged on the ability of the present generation of sons to produce a male heir in order to inherit the family wealth. It was proving a difficult task and the *telenovela* presented a series of discourses on male sexuality which were organised around the main character and his inability to produce an heir. Thus, a familiar theme was also moving the discussion of sexualities across boundaries and away from women towards men. The dilemmas remained unresolved, essential for the success of the programme, but the drama was sustained by the issues of sexualities, class relations, imperialism and the nation.

In Ecuador the most popular *telenovela* in 1994 was *Guadalupe*, a Mexican import that again used all the conventions of the genre. The central character Guadalupe was the illegitimate daughter of a beautiful but maltreated domestic within a wealthy family who sets out to avenge her mother and restore her honour. First, via marriage to the wealthy Alfredo which proves disastrous and second, via success in business which, despite any depiction of what might be construed as a working day, seems to succeed. *Guadalupe* raised issues of divorce, single parenthood, women alone and tackled rape and the physical abuse of women by men. The terrain for this discussion was a wealthy, upper-middle-class milieu, belying the fiction that violence against women is an issue of poverty and the working class. As popular television it was enormously successful because it was visually exciting and packed with passion and drama that related to issues constructed as fundamental rather than trivial. The audience was not patronised but invited to be part of a debate on serious contemporary issues. This debate was made possible by the lack of fixity between viewers, readers and characters constructing a space of dissent into which people could insert themselves and contribute as knowing subjects. This 'space of dissent' also organised an articulation between the home as a site of cultural consumption and the imaginary of the nation. The two became one through the correlative imaginaries of viewers/subjects discursively constructed via the ensuing debates. The importance of this cannot be underestimated. These processes test out specific commonsense understandings in circulation, like the issues around male violence foregrounded by *Guadalupe*, and rupture the 'naturalisation' of accepted views. In so doing people see themselves and their views in the mirror of the nation.

Telenovelas provide a collective space for the nation in several ways linked to the discussion of national space/time. The Colombian series, *Café*, and others from Brazil, Mexico and Argentina offer a vision of the historical and social development of a specific nation-state drawing the viewer into a story which becomes a form of both individual and collective cultural capital interacting with historical time and the geographic and social space of the nation. This was transparent in *Café* where viewers could immediately connect with the sign *Café* as a signifier of Colombia and the political and economic importance of coffee in the past, present and future of the country. Yet these dramatised histories were organised around production values which emphasise visual impact and human interest stories, most importantly, seduction and betrayal in love and business. Nevertheless, *Café* offered a 'telespace' shared by millions at the same time, week after week, in which Colombians engaged with a vision of their past and present society sustaining a powerful interpellation. But there was little attention to issues of racism and exploitation in the development of Colombia.

However, it is possible to view the main narrative as a tale in which the poor and dispossessed (embodied in the main female character Carolina and as Guadalupe) were represented and shown to be active in their attempts to right injustice and claim a place in the nation. *Telenovelas* offer a narrative and characters that are shared by millions (both women and men) and that are referenced in other media forms. This form of intertextuality further reinforces the sense of a national story and identity, a sort of living history of the nation in which everyone, via television, can take part. Ecuador is an interesting case in relation to these observations because it has not had a national *telenovela*. *Telenovelas* are imported, currently from Mexico, Colombia and previously from the Southern cone states. This does not mean that the space of the national is denuded but that the millions who watched *Guadalupe* engaged with a Mexican *telenovela* produced on location in Miami. The shared space of television, evidenced in news broadcasts, current affairs programmes and *telenovelas*, does not, however, provide a shared interpretation – this is fractured and contested by class, 'race', gender and regional and political positionalities. Thus, the integrative work of television in the production of a 'national culture' is a constant process of mediation, tentative, unstable and lacking in fixity. The centring project of television in any nation-state is also undermined by the globalisation of cultural products which suggests different transnational constituencies.

The power of mass popular culture has not been so easily understood by either the Left generally or the indigenous movement in Ecuador as it has been by the Right and the current generation of politicians. The cultural moment for these groups has been set up in opposition to mass popular culture. For example, CONAIE organised an indigenous, first nations video and film festival using some powerful historical and contemporary material from the archives to the moment of the 1990 Uprisings. The 1990 Uprisings were a precursor to the more recent power of the organisation and brought CONAIE to the attention of the global media. Members marched from every part of

Ecuador and converged in the capital city Quito where the collective strength of the organisation reclaimed streets and squares and disrupted the legislatures. Sadly, few people attended the event in Quito; the reason for the poor turnout was acknowledged to be a clash with two very important televised football matches that were part of the World Cup qualifying rounds.

In an earlier clash with football, in the summer of 1993, CONAIE leaders, frustrated by their discussions with government on land reform, walked out of the discussions and threatened to disrupt the *Copa América* which was being hosted by Ecuador. This threat was greeted with derision by a hostile press and constructed as an example of the distance between the indigenous movement and the popular concerns of Ecuadoreans, celebrated as the hosts of the *Copa*. The newspaper and television coverage allowed the media to negatively construct difference in relation to the indigenous movement. The movement was out of touch, 'non-modern' and thereby the leadership of the movement was distanced from 'the people'. CONAIE, however, is too powerful and confident to be troubled by negative press coverage but it did encourage some of the leaders of the movement, themselves football fans, to reconsider the role of mass popular culture in the struggle for indigenous rights.

Footballing nations

Football is a passion in Latin America and matches are alive with music, banners, songs and chants. It is this joy in football that was imported into the US for the 1994 World Cup with Mexican waves, carnival style Brazilian costumes and the atmosphere of a street party. Football is also megabucks, politics and corruption so tragically played out in relation to the Colombian team, one of whom, Andrés Escobar, was shot following a disastrous performance in the 1994 World Cup. Life for footballers is gentler in Ecuador but power and money in relation to national pride is a highly charged cocktail.

Ecuador is not one of the major footballing nations of Latin America – it has yet to produce a team with the flair of the ill-fated Colombian team or players of the brilliance of Pélé or Maradona. However, one of the teams from Guayaquil, Barcelona, has done well in Latin American tournaments and there is no lack of enthusiasm for the sport. When Ecuador was knocked out of the 1994 World Cup qualifying rounds at an early stage there was deep mourning and extended media coverage of the defeat and the reasons for Ecuador's performance. National pride was at stake and large sections of the population mourned the end of Ecuador's World Cup career. But Ecuadoreans cheerfully and generously shifted their loyalty to Colombia and pinned their hopes on their neighbour, especially after Colombia beat Argentina 5–0 in Buenos Aires.

While football does reinforce class and regional loyalties, offering symbols of cities and localities, it offers a clear focal point for national discourses because football teams have come to symbolise national pride and shame. These are deeply felt emotions tied to conceptions that individuals have of the life of the nation and some hazy notion of 'national destiny'. What this means for nations and national identities in the modern era is that football, too, constitutes and marks conceptions of time and space. The game of football is itself a product of modernity, bound to disciplinary modes that have been codified this century. The discursive space of the game is rule-bound via local, national and international finance and institutions. It is the global game transported from Europe, played across the world, remade and revisioned as it has travelled. (See Archetti, 1994, for a discussion of Argentinian national sentiments and the role of football.)

Football generates a sense of national time and space from the popular rather than the official histories of the nation; although football can clearly bring the two together in the most manipulative ways, for example the staging of the World Cup in Argentina in 1978, where the generals decided that football could be used as a unifying project in a fascist state. It backfired and the media coverage sent images of the *Madres*, the Mothers of the Disappeared of the *Plaza de Mayo*, protesting the loss of their children and their disappearance from the national consciousness around the world.

The national boundaries generated by football and the ways in which they are transgressed offer a symbolic space into which people can insert themselves and where their identities can be called up as individuals and as part of the collective subject of the nation. This sense of belonging is located not just in the present but in a past, a past of tragedies and triumphs, trophies won and lost, and where national pride is foregrounded. It is precisely because it is an emotional space, a romance, an affair of the heart, that it is so powerful (Westwood, 1991). This does not mean that it is always positive. Such moments can also produce a murderous and violent nationalism that has been seen in Europe. The history of the nation is reinterpreted and dated by a series of World Cup successes in Argentina and Brazil. Thus, it is precisely in the arena of global international competition that the game of football is so prominent and so clearly reinforces the imaginary of the nation.

However, while presented as a democratic and popular arena which belongs to all, 'the people's game', the politics and economics of football show clearly that the story is much more complex. Yet, football is still privileged as a narrator of the nation. The narrator in question is masculine and football is a romance built around an idealised masculinity, as Archetti (1994) elaborates in relation to Argentina. Even this, however, is full of contradiction, as exemplified in the life and times of Maradona, so different from those of Pélé. The social and ethnic backgrounds of these two men fuel the romance of football while simultaneously silencing issues of racism and class exploitation, generating national stories that produce national heroes from below. At the popular level, they mirror the processes of nation-formation with its horizontal integration and symbolic ownership of heroes. It is these processes that are in play in what I have called 'correlative imaginaries' where identities are placed in a space or site such as football on the basis of a correlation of the self with the social which imagines mutual intelligibility, even though the interests of managers, players, financiers and spectators may be economically and politically antagonistic. However, the processes of identification are not impeded because football is understood as a part of popular culture and a realm of creativity and freedom. This is, in part, a fiction but a necessary fiction in relation to the ability of football to symbolise the nation and national destiny. Correlative imaginaries place national and individual destinies side by side, the one with the other, as a powerful evocation of a 'correlative destiny'.

Conclusion

This chapter has sought ways in which to tease out an understanding of the ways in which 'political love' is generated and sustained in the form of national loyalties and sentiments. While Anderson's contentious notion was seen to be expressed in the form of poetry, song, music and writing alongside the emotional bonds to the nation, this discussion has sought ways in the Latin American context to reframe both the notion of 'political love' and its expression. This chapter has sought to elaborate an alternative conceptualisation in 'correlative imaginaries' in the context of popular cultural forms. By concentrating upon the popular it is possible to foreground the fragility of correlative imaginaries as a coalescence of the expression of national sentiments. Popular religion is another site in which the processes of identification and a sense of belonging are powerfully nurtured both in popular Catholicism and the growth of the new Protestant churches in Latin America (Lehman, 1996). These elements of popular culture are central to the configurations that come to be known as national identities, offering narratives of time and space with which people can connect emotionally and psychologically. The importance of these spaces of belonging for the imaginaries of national identities cannot be underestimated. They offer, like the construction of 'the family', mediations between local and national, big and small worlds. Mediations that have been discussed in this chapter in relation to television and, I have suggested, the importance of the *telenovela* which constructs national time and space and a sphere of cultural capital which, like football at the national level, is open to all. These modern forms provide the spaces within which individuals can frame correlative imaginaries between themselves and the imaginary community of the nation. At the symbolic level the schisms and diversity which multiply and decentre the social and the nation constituting a politics of belonging are suspended in relation to a symbolic inclusivity, in effect, a romance of belonging which is the national story.

Chapter 3

The politics of belonging

Imagining America, remembering home: Latino/a cultures in urban America

Sallie Westwood

> We find ground on which to make our stand. ... Among the great
> struggles of man – good/evil, reason/unreason, etc. – there is also
> the mighty conflict between the fantasy of Home and the fantasy of
> Away, the dreams of roots and the mirage of the journey.
>
> (Rushdie, 1999: 55)

Introduction

While the national story invokes a grand narrative of belonging into
which citizens are inducted and which, it has been suggested, is
experienced in much more specific moments, the emphasis of late has
been upon the transnational. The discourses in which the space of the
transnational is generated are examined by Portes (1999) and Vertovec
(1999) in an attempt to delineate a social field. Portes reproduces
many of the earlier accounts from migration studies, discussed in
greater depth in the later chapters of this book. Vertovec is more
conscious of the impact of studies of diasporas and the postnational
through the work of Hall (1990, 1991) and Appadurai (1995) but,
nevertheless, retains the migratory perspective. In many respects this
reproduces the grand narratives of nation-state formations – migrants
move from one to the other, reproducing a binary which is perhaps less
useful in trying to understand the new social spaces of global, diasporic
cities in which hybrid cultures are being fashioned. The importance of
context for the production of the political, economic and cultural
spaces of transnationality is emphasised by Guarnizo, Sánchez and
Roach (1999) in their study of Colombians in the cities of New York

and Los Angeles, suggesting that the urban and the specificities of the cityscapes in which transnational lives are lived is a crucial component of our understanding. In this chapter the emphasis on urban cultures reproduces their concerns. Equally, the binary of nation and migration reproduces a commonsense understanding of stasis and mobility already punctured by writers like Stuart Hall and Zigmunt Bauman in their emphasis upon mobility in all our lives. There is another difficulty with this binary and that is the homogeneity that is afforded the category of the nation-state, reproducing the official rhetoric of nation-building and ignoring the fractured, decentred world of nation-states, elaborated in the previous chapters. Nowhere is this more apparent than in the nation-states of Latin America. Thirdly, the construction of the nation and migration as a binary ignores the development of nations in an historically globalised world in which nation-states have shared histories. Again, nowhere is this more salient than in the Americas and that is an essential part of the understanding of the politics of belonging in this chapter.

'I want to be in America' – the familiar refrain from the musical *West Side Story* contains both dreams of consumption and a critique of the folk wisdom that constitutes 'America' as the land of abundance available to all. As James Donald (1992) wrote in relation to the city, 'there is no such *thing* as a city', equally there is no such 'thing' as a nation-state, a country, and yet it is constantly produced and reproduced through the imaginings of the peoples within and beyond the borders. Rather like Walter Benjamin's call to read cities as texts comprising a multitude of stories so, too, we can attempt to reconstruct the imaginaries of nations and the place of the urban within these imaginings.

The imagining of the USA and of Latin America constitutes a two-way process in which, not surprisingly, the US is constructed as a land of things to be bought and sold, of high technology, wealth and power for many in Latin America. It is constituted, as the film showed, as '*el Norte*', part of a binary between the poverty and hardship of the South and the opportunities and money of the North. It is a space geographically somewhere to the North encompassing the 'rest of the world'. It is only on arrival that the complexities of this space become apparent. From the North, Latin America is constructed and read as both exotic, with shamans and ancient peoples defending the Amazonian forest, and as a place of corruption, generals and drug cartels which needs policing by the ever-vigilant US military, CIA and agents of the state department. But, even within this imaginary, there are fractures and from within civil society groups of human rights activists, of aid workers and musicians and artists who make distinctive connections within Latin America. While both of the hegemonic visions have long histories, it is the age of television which has made such an impact and it is, in part, a televisual imagination which provides the texture and nuance to these constructions of, on the one hand, the land of plenty – 'God's own country' – and, on the other, the land of corruption, poverty and hard times. A major factor in the more recent Latin American view is the impact of the Miami-based *telenovelas* which are made for the Spanish-speaking Latin American market. Many depict the good life in Miami or Mexico City with large houses, large cars, lots of food, shopping malls, servants and, of course, like most soap operas, little hint of work. For the migrant, on the other hand, paid work is the reason for moving and comes to fill the spaces of the North in terms of the trajectories of migration.

The imaginings of these territorially governed spaces of nation-states are, however, powerfully undermined by popular cultures and the forms of cultural capitalism that trade in music, film and television. Latin America hosts the same huge pop concerts held in the cities of the US and imports rock music and jazz while it exports salsa, son, tango, rock music recast with a Latin beat like the Mexican band Maná, jazz musicians and those who use indigenous rhythms recast for the global market – Carlos Vives, for example, or Los Lobos. Ricky Martin recycles and reaffirms the popularity of the 'Latin' beat in rock and roll. Globo television from Brazil exports programmes and personalities like Xuxa to the US. In this circulation of sounds and commodities an alternative account of the imaginary of Latin America is produced which encourages the possibility of exploring the ethnic and cultural diversity of Latin America – that 'outsized reality' as Gabriel García Márquez has called this imaginary. Novelists also play a role in the ways in which the exotic is privileged, having created a whole genre of magical realism which is copied, tried out and used globally. It has been appropriated most successfully by Indian writers writing in English (Salman Rushdie and Arundhati Roy for example). Compare the complexity of this form with the pulp fiction of books like *Body of*

Truth, a thriller set in Guatemala. Latterly, a new genre of 'diasporic', Latin American writing is being created by young novelists like Junot Díaz. Cultural products offer the possibility of a decolonisation of the imagination despite the power of television to construct images of 'the other' and recycle the myths of Latin America and of the USA.

Borders

Against the globalisation of cultural products and the commodification of specific arts and crafts there is the commodification of whole nations through the tourist trade. This is a trade which offers sun, sex, and pleasure as well as the opportunity to consume Aztec ruins, old Mexico, haciendas and the folkloric worlds of Latin America. These imaginings and the tourist trade do, at one level, also differentiate the world of Latino culture into nation-states with borders, cultures and geographical features. The tourists who travel to Ecuador to visit the Galapagos Islands visit an Ecuador not much travelled by Ecuadoreans themselves who are more likely to belong to an urban world whether of the coast or the highlands. Part of this urban world, especially for the middle classes, looks to the USA for employment opportunities, training, consumption patterns and style and reproduces this within the cities of Latin America. High-rise blocks in Quito and Cali are modelled in part on Miami, notwithstanding the maids' quarters which are still included in the architecture of middle-class enclaves. Similarly, houses are hybrid in style, matching Spanish colonial style with US 'dens', basements and plumbing. This is a two-way process evidenced in the middle-class enclaves of California where the same Spanish styles are commonplace. While these ideas travel, people from the nation-states of Latin America face 'the border' and US immigration control, as aliens and subject to the indignities of immigration control. This is part of the globalisation process – a process which moves not just capital and commodities around the world but also people as Sassen (1996) and Bauman (1998) emphasise. The borders that greet people in Miami or Texas or California are policed in ways that the borders of Latin American nation-states are not in relation to the incursions of the multinationals, especially the oil companies in Amazonia that now have interests in shrimp fishing (BP) and other basic utilities like power, water, minerals, previously acknowledged to be 'national resources'.

These economic incursions have not been effected without contestations – demonstrations in Ecuador, law suits against Texaco, and guerrilla groups in Colombia who regularly blow up the pipelines.

The US is everywhere in Latin America but it is also clear that Latin America is everywhere in the US. Miami is a bilingual city as are parts of Chicago, Los Angeles and New York. Colombia's independence day is celebrated in the huge Flushing Meadows Corona Park in Queens in New York City. 'It is a truly transnational celebration and one that has been held every summer since 1985. With the exception of the organizers, the Colombian consul and Miss Colombia, none of the speakers was Colombian' (Guarnizo *et al.*, 1999: 368). There has been historically, and continues to be, a mirror dance between the two Americas. One step in the dance is the constant transgression of borders – through the increasing numbers of people who enter the US both legally and illegally. It was suggested in 1995, for example, that New York had more than 14,000 illegal Ecuadoreans (*New York Times*). Given the size of Ecuador, with a population of ten million at the last census, whatever the truth or falsehood of the above figure, it gives some idea of the mobility of Ecuadoreans and that the Latin American population throughout the US is growing apace. In part this is the outcome of the global economy but it is also the large numbers of second and third generation US-born people of Latin American descent who now make their home in the cities of the US. Puerto Ricans are already US citizens but it is estimated that Latinos (classified in the US census as Hispanics) will outnumber the black population in the next ten years (as they do currently in twenty-one states) and that they comprise 27 per cent of the workforce and 14 per cent of the population, some 20 million people, and continuing to rise. It is also clear that this population is an increasingly diverse population.

Living the imaginary

When I was living in Quito I rented a flat from Cecilia who owned a hotel, flats and property in the city and in the town of Otavalo, famous for its market, tourism and crafts which are sold globally. I asked Cecilia where she felt she belonged and to which country, where was her '*patria chica*'. Cecilia had spent twenty years in Miami and replied that she was both Ecuadorean and American and that America was her '*patria chica*', as much her home, 'maybe more so', than Quito or Otavalo. Similarly, friends in Colombia who had studied in the US always spoke of their 'American families' with whom they maintained ongoing and close ties over decades. In these cases individuals saw no borders and the 'Americas' were all part of one world.

It is often very different for rural migrants or those from the small towns of Mexico who come to the US to work in the fields. Using 1997 census data and the work of Gelbard and Carter (1997), Roberts, Frank and Lozano-Ascencio (1999: 240) suggest that Mexicans account for 14 per cent of documented migrants and 40 per cent of undocumented and that immigrants account for 37 per cent of the Mexican descent population in the US, an estimated 7,017,000 or 27 per cent of the foreign-born population. As labour they move from California to Texas to work in tomato fields where the crop has been engineered and organised for the forms of imported labour that these migrants constitute. The ties that they have to their home towns are strong and they have obligations in the form of community roles and service, political office, families, and a sense of home outside the US (Besserer, 1998). Migrants like these from Mexico are important both to the Mexican economy and the US economy. Many learn Spanish and English in the US because they speak an indigenous language in a specific local dialect and they come to occupy a series of spaces that are not binational but are better understood as multicentric. The place of work may be California or they are moved to Texas, but for many of the workers, earning below the minimum wage, places in 'America' are not designated or named, they are all part of 'the tomatoes'. 'The tomatoes' defines places by the products that the workers sustain.

In other ways migrants have forged a sense of home in the unpromising borderlands of the Rio Grande through the formation of *colonias*, a form of self-help housing known throughout Latin America and often the consequence of land invasions which are then recognised and services developed. In Texas alone some 400,000 people are living in these settlements without services although they have legal rights in the land as long as they continue to pay the mortgage. If there is a default on the loan the developer takes it all back. These are areas way beyond city borders that provide an answer to the housing needs of migrant workers but they do not have the community base of the Mexican version and the state of Texas does not view these housing developments as a rational response to poverty, low wages and lack of access to housing. Instead, the state has pathologised the inhabitants and learned only to use the term *colonias* in a derogatory fashion. However, as Ward (1999) has suggested, other sections of the poorest people in Texas are also looking at these settlements as an improvement on trailer parks and a possible way forward for themselves. The state of Texas with no housing policy is blind to the social capital within the *colonias* and the potential for self-organisation on the Mexican model. Ward and his colleagues have been involved in a state-sponsored study in which they are encouraging Texas to learn from Mexico. Another example of the mirror-dance between the two Americas.

The residents of the *colonias* are the rural migrants who provide material for the ways in which Latino/a peoples and cultures are constructed and represented in the US. However, it is within the urban spaces that the cities of North America are being made over by the growing presence of Spanish-speaking peoples. The growing bilingualism of cities and states in the US has been racialised in particular ways, generating a nationwide organisation for the hegemony of the English language – a form of cultural defence it is claimed against the growing 'threat' from Spanish (Urcioli, 1997). The growing sense of a Hispanic world within the cities has generated hostility and a new hierarchy of ethnicities in which 'chicanos' and 'Latinos' are the new 'others' of the urban landscape. In this process diversity is conflated and homogenised and individuals come to stand in for a category – to represent the Spanish-speaking alien. The lived reality with its texture and nuance is very different.

The Latin presence in American cities has come to know and lay claims to these urban landscapes and to create homes and a sense of belonging within this. Puerto Ricans, speaking Spanish and sharing both a Latin and a Caribbean culture, have, suggests Sciorra (1996), contributed to the 'caribbeanisation' of New York, most especially through the reclamation of parts of the South Bronx in which Puerto Ricans have built, on derelict land, the kind of small houses, *casita*, reminiscent of the island of Puerto Rico with two or three rooms and a veranda. When a fire destroyed much of this in 1990 people in the locality came together to rebuild the area. This is an importation of vernacular architecture which changes the visual and aesthetic spaces of the urban, contributing to the sense of a hybrid, diasporic spatial aesthetic. The remaking of housing, just like the dance halls and Friday night celebrations, are part of a remembering which is active, not simply a nostalgia for the familiarity of home but an attempt to make a home in a new landscape.

This new landscape, especially in New York, is fuelled by the rise of the global city which has had a major impact on the ethnoscape of the city with the arrival of more migrants from Latin America and South-East Asia. This has also meant the gentrification of parts of the city (comparable with London) in which the poor and dispossessed are usurped from the marginal spaces they claimed as their own. One example of this, discussed by Neil Smith as an example of the 'revanchist city', was the struggle over Tompkins Square on the Lower East Side in New York in which the homeless were removed from the park in part by a Neighbourhood Association which included developers, homeowners and Antonio Pagan, a Latino property developer, who came to lead the coalition against the homeless, housing for people with aids, and a drug rehabilitation unit. Although out as a gay man, Pagan found himself opposed by both sections of the gay community and by 'a coalition of progressive Latinos'. The park was reopened but as part of the gentrified Lower East Side and Pagan's victory was secured in the 1993 elections (Smith, 1996). The story of Tompkins Square also elaborates the fractures within the Latino population and the cultural and political remixing that is current. This is a politics of urban America not concerned, as the Cuban population in Miami, with struggles over the places from which migrants have migrated. The Cuban population in the US is a very specific population held together by the ongoing war with Fidel Castro.

For those who are not professionals or students the inner city is the fabric within which a sense of place is built and this has been the source of often fierce contestations in relation to the territorialisation of urban spaces. The most celebrated expressions of this politics of space and belonging are to be found in the gangs of young men who contest spaces with other gangs in the neighbourhood. Some of these contestations bring young black men into conflict with young Latino men over space but also over resources, income and trade. Many Latinos now occupy positions once occupied by sections of the black population – from workers in agriculture to routine manual work. But within the cities there are myriad ways to generate income and many are not related to a job in the conventional sense. Ducking and diving, trading in goods, casualised forms of work are the mainstay of life. The public spaces of the urban are fought over and won, defended and lost in an ongoing attempt to exercise power in the spaces of the locale. These are the spaces of diaspora and transnationalism, producing a complex ethnic politics consistent with the ethnoscapes of urban America. It is also a predominantly masculine and youth struggle over 'turf', forms of nationalism of the neighbourhood recognisable in the UK as much as the US. These processes are also constitutive of identities, local, ethnic and city-based, in which the struggles provide locations constantly in need of policing, defending and reasserting by the different gangs.

This is a very different route to a sense of home and belonging from that produced by sections of the population coming together in churches, dance halls and associations, some of which link places of origin to the new milieu while others are concerned to foster a sense of place within the cities of the US. The notion of home is complex and contains within it the sense of loss and of the new, but for one group of workers it is more ambivalent. These are the women who come to the US as domestic workers contributing through their labour to the reproduction of the households of the middle classes, predominantly the white middle classes, but not exclusively so. The maids, carers of children and the elderly live within the space of the home, but are simultaneously outside the family and home of their employers in a relational and emotional sense. Many of these women, like the women working in the factories, are sending money 'home', that is, back to Mexico or Guatemala in order to assist family, buy bricks or land to build a house. Some women do return, but many 'develop ineradicable ties over time to the communities where they live and work in the United States' (Repack, 1997: 256). The differences between household strategies are explored in a paper by Fernandez-Kelly and Garcia (1997) on Cuban and Mexican women working in factories in Florida and California. The Cuban women in Florida had a very high rate of economic activity and worked in relation to a household strategy aimed at raising family income for education, consumer durables and generally increasing standards of living and household capital. In contrast, Mexican women in California were more likely to be heads of households or members of relatively impoverished households where their earnings were crucial to subsistence. These differences are repeated throughout the US and contribute either to the developing differentiations by class of the Latin American descent populations in the country or to the consolidations of class distinctions within the populations.

Diasporic politics

The Latin American entrants to the US come from the racialised, diasporic spaces of the nation-states of the region in which European, Jewish, Palestinian and Japanese, to name some of the ethnicities familiar throughout Latin America, are part of a world in which hybridity and *mestizaje* are the official ideology of nation-building. As the earlier chapters have elaborated, states in Latin America do not collect statistics on ethnicity within the national censuses. Officially *mestizaje* marks the racial mixture which is common throughout but, while the ideology suggests this is a democratic conception, it is actually allied with a hierarchy of colour denoting race, with white at the apex. The ideology is, in fact, about valorising whitening and whiteness rather than racial mixture. Thus, sections of the Mexican social formation claiming indigenous roots, speaking an indigenous language rather than Spanish, are not part of the imaginary of the Mexican nation (Mallon, 1995). The United States, with its legally sanctioned individual freedoms, discourse of rights and democratic traditions, is, however, no less a vehicle for the valorisation of whiteness and is marked by the binary black/white against which black people have fought for the vote, for civil rights and for recognition as part of the nation. Thus, migrants are moving from one racialised diasporic space into another with some easily recognised attributes, racism against black people, the decimation of the indigenous peoples and a complex ethnoscape of Italians, Greeks, Asians, Jews, South Asians and many more who may or may not be identified by a hyphenated designation, for example, 'Jewish-American'. Culturally complex, the officially celebrated melting pot, has welded diversity, rather than hybridity, into an account of white American identity which has been fostered over decades. Latin Americans come into a space in which they are homogenised and through this marginalised and offered a place on the periphery. Further, coming into a city like Miami, which saw the Hispanic population rise rapidly in a decade, Latinos/as face the white backlash deflected through the issue of language. The Latinisation of Miami happened very quickly, from 5.3 per cent of the population in 1960 to 35.7 per cent in 1980 (Castro, 1997). During this time the Latin population has secured a place in the economy not just as manual workers but as entrepreneurs. While the official ideology was assimilationist and Dade county gave official recognition to the state as bicultural and bilingual in 1973, by 1980 the white backlash had organised the English Only campaign which they took onto the national stage later in the decade. The black population of Miami, viewing this as racially motivated, was lukewarm despite the difficulties that some sections of the black population had encountered through competition for jobs, housing and health care (Castro, 1997). Sections of the black population were more organised and directly hostile to the arrival of Nicaraguan migrants and refugees in Miami. In South Central Los Angeles there has been a number of violent encounters between young men from black and Latino gangs fighting for control of the locality. However, the gangs succeeded in calling a truce and coming together against the LAPD (Los Angeles Police Department) when the graffiti announced 'Crips, Bloods, Mexicans. Together. Forever. Tonite' [*sic*] with 'LAPD' crossed out and '187' underneath.

Ambivalence marks many of these encounters and coalitions are fragile and often contingent. Nevertheless, it is the lack of fixity that produces outcomes that are not determinate, as recent accounts illustrate. Flores (1997) explores the ways in which Puerto Rican and African American young people share rap and graffiti, dance forms and social space in New York which promotes a 'growing together' out of which comes a sense of 'AmeRican' or in the cityscape of New York, 'Nuyoricans' as new transnational identities. The suggestion is that the Caribbean cultural mix of Puerto Rico creates a basis for the coming together of black Americans and Puerto Ricans especially among the young men. Flores' account is not gendered in the sense of suggesting the ways in which masculinities are recognisable between these groups compared with the situation for girls and women and the social constructions of femininity in the North American context. The account of New York does suggest the fluidity and malleability of ethnic identities in the city and the importance of the spatial in producing cultural identities.

One facet of popular culture not much explored is the role of sport in Latino/a ethnic identifications and the articulation between the hyphen of hyphenated US identities. The staging of the World Cup in 1994 provided a space for soccer enthusiasts from Latin America to show the United States what soccer was all about, why it is a passion and in what ways it could be promoted. Although volleyball, basketball and baseball are also played throughout the Latin American states nothing excites the passionate response, the carnivalesque atmosphere and spectacle in the way that soccer does. Young Latinos kick soccer balls in neighbourhoods throughout US cities to Latin rhythms from the surrounding windows and cars. Despite Pélé's performances for the New York Cosmos in the late 1970s and the revival of Major League Soccer in 1992, the big money has not yet bought into soccer, so what is a passion, as it is for kids throughout Latin American cities, and world-wide, cannot yet be traded and turned into a career with the kind of rewards available to American football, baseball and basketball players.

Diasporic politics is worked through within the complex eth-noscapes of the urban in the US in which in a variety of sites identities are made and reframed in the processes of interaction. In the factories, for example, where racism positions Mexicans or Puerto Ricans as 'Latinos/as' or 'chicanos/as'. Latino/a workers are ideologically constituted as different within a racial hierarchy that places them below white workers and this is expressed materially through the hours, the anti-social shifts and the low pay. These differentials may be recast in the neighbourhood through the power of young men to police their space and claim it as their own. Equally important are the churches and the attempt to generate and sustain community, integrity and status in a hostile environment. Food cultures become acts of resistance and an antidote to corporate America's corruption found in 'Tex/Mex' and Tacobel. Schooling, healthcare, the criminal justice system and the institutional nexus of US states present rules for living, regimes through which all sections of society are inducted into the national codes, national space and time. These are forms of governance in which the outcomes are uncertain and may have unintended conse-quences for conceptions of the citizen and the consumer.

However, it is within the realms of popular culture, from the *Teatro Viva* of Los Angeles in which gay and lesbian Latinos/as tackled the issue of AIDS, to the singers and poets, rap artists and musicians, writers and artists, that some part of the engagement with the US can be found. This encounter is already reframing both Latin and 'American' identities, especially among young people. It can be seen in the play with language, the witty 'AmeRican' which is placing the new generations in the urban world of the cityscape. Equally, it is present in the writing of Junot Diáz who, in the short story 'How to Date a Browngirl, Blackgirl, Whitegirl or Halfie', writes, 'She'll say, I like Spanish guys, and even though you've never been to Spain, say, I like you. You'll sound smooth.'

The new ethnicities of the urban world of US cities, of New York and Chicago, Los Angeles and Washington, are part of a much older story in which cities have been racialised. From the earliest period of settlements cities have been decentred through the delineation of racialised space. But this spatial pattern which constitutes for so many the 'geographies of exclusion' (Sibley, 1995) is also part of the imaginary of cities which brings the social and subjectivities together (Westwood, 1997). It is this story of racialised space which is undermined by the graffiti – 'Crips, Bloods, Mexicans. Forever. Tonite' [sic] – which is also a response to the forms of racism which police 'the others' of the city through modes of constant surveillance which make black people and people with their origins in Latin America constantly visible within a discourse of racism constituted in time and space. Surveillance is exercised in relation to the Latino/a population in relation to the discourse of migration and the construction of 'the illegal' who is an ever-present threat to the borders of the United States, to order and to whiteness as part of the American dream. It is, as many from the Latin American states discover, a racialised dream and one in which they are not imagined. This does not, however, halt the production of dreams. Dreams, ideals, are reframed in the cities of the US within the development of vibrant, complex and resistant Latin cultures where people, while remembering home, are creating their own sense of belonging in 'el Norte'.

Chapter 4

Economic ethnoscapes

'Diamonds are forever': ethnicity, economy and the Indian diamond trade

Sallie Westwood

The setting for this chapter moves attention away from the Latin American context to South Asia, more specifically to India and the Indian diamond trade. Diamonds, however, are an important sign of a globalised world and the ways in which raw materials are claimed by nations and used by capitalist transnational companies within a global marketing strategy. The national and the global are articulated in specific ways in relation to the diamond trade and some part of these processes are explored in this chapter. While the narrative concentrates attention upon diamond dealers within India it is clear that they are part of an international story that involves the movements of people alongside goods. This is, however, a complex story which requires a sociology which is indeed 'beyond societies' in which mobility of labour and vision are co-extensive and in which cultures as the practice of ethnicities and genders have an important part to play.

There is a developing literature within sociology on the processes of globalisation (King, 1991; Said, 1993; Turner, 1994; Lash and Urry, 1994; Featherstone *et al.*, 1995; Urry, 2000) in which ethnicities and cultural practices are foregrounded. Equally, there has been an attempt to analyse the meanings of the market and to reconsider the embeddedness of economic relations in social processes (see, for example, Granovetter, 1985; Friedland and Robertson, 1990; Dilley, 1992; Carrier, 1995). In this chapter I am going to examine the articulations between these spheres as constitutive of the diamond trade and seek to tease out and analyse the complex relations that construct this sphere.

There is a popular literature (see Green, 1981) including 'coffee table' books on 'the romance of diamonds', but little economic and sociological literature on the diamond trade. There is a large literature on the Jewish diaspora and one account (Yogdev, 1978) of the historical role of Jews in the Indian diamond trade. Equally, there are extant accounts of the South African diamond sector (Pallister *et al.*, 1987) and the story of De Beers (Kanfer, 1993) and a recent account (Laidlaw, 1995) of the Jains as gem dealers in India. More generally, however, the literature on the Jains and the Jain diaspora is sparse (see Carrithers and Humphrey, 1991; Banks, 1992). However, there is a large literature on the Indian economy and more recently on the processes of economic liberalisation (Joshi and Little, 1996, for example) and the current situation in *Fortune India*, *India Today*, *Economic and Political Weekly*, etc.

Diamonds were mined in India in what is currently Andhra Pradesh throughout the sixteenth and seventeenth centuries as the main source until diamonds were discovered in Brazil in 1725. Muslim rulers used the rough stones as ornaments but also to ward off evil and protect the wearer. As the quality of the diamonds was measured by the hardness they were worn by men and associated with masculine values. Cutting and polishing techniques were very rudimentary and often the stone was simply hung around the neck. It was not until the eighteenth century that diamond cutting was developed in Antwerp and Amsterdam. It was in these cities that the diamond trade flourished and the technologies associated with diamond cutting developed within the tight-knit communities of Jewish urban dwellers. It is also clear that through history and into the twentieth century, as the trade in diamonds grew, diamonds were associated with royalty and the aristocracy. A quick scan of the Rijksmuseum in Amsterdam shows portraits of wealthy burghers wearing pearls. The only possible exception to this, and it is not clear, is Rembrandt's *The Jewish Wedding*. This is, as far as I am aware, true of the English landed aristocracy of Gainsborough's portraits. Diamonds were the preserve of Indian princes and some sections of European royalty.

The modern diamond trade

Current enthusiasm for globalisation and transnationalism is often ahistorical, a form of forgetting an earlier era when monopolies in relation to raw materials were set up in conditions of unequal exchange. The diamond trade as it developed did so in a thoroughly modern way located with global trade and diasporic populations in an era of monopolies that pre-date the power of transnational corporations but also provide a model of integrated production and marketing. Basically, the rise of the diamond trade is the story of De Beers and the consolidation of the cartel, the Central Selling Organisation, which organises the flow of diamonds between producers and sellers. The story of De Beers, recently popularised through the overblown TV production, *Rhodes*, is, like the present situation, a story alive with rogues and heroes, transnational risk taking and entrepreneurial flair. The trade is also known for its secrecy and the way in which trust relations are crucial to the exchange of goods and money. The power struggles over control of the mines and then the trade have added to the allure of diamonds which in their uncut state are barely distinguishable from rock salt or white quartz. The romance of diamonds has always been there in the stories of magical properties and the association with wealth and men of honour, the princes. But the modern industry of the twentieth century has recast this romance, weaving it into the global marketing of diamonds and the sustenance of profits.

Diamonds have become objects of desire in an unprecedented way in the twentieth century within the context of heterosexual romantic love seemingly made to stand in for, to signify, enduring love which, like a diamond, cannot be shattered and is as individual as the shimmering stone. As if to turn history on its head diamonds have been sold to women as a gift from men – men may come and go but 'a diamond is forever' and, while it is possible to burn or shatter a diamond, few recipients at the end of a relationship opt for this. Instead, in the modern era diamonds have been used as part of the betrothal of couples as engagement rings, a very modern phenomenon, and in eternity rings or in wedding rings all of which signify love between a man and a woman. This modern variant has been slow to catch on in Germany for example or in Japan but it now has. It is the USA which has done so much to promote diamond jewellery on this model and not surprisingly, it was in New York in 1938 that the De Beers slogan, 'a diamond is forever', was coined. It tells us something about the power of words as signs that this more than anything is what the popular imagination sees when it sees diamonds. Latterly, and consistent with the postmodern turn and niche marketing, De Beers has a series of differential marketing strategies – women in Japan and South-East Asia are just as likely, given the necessary income, to buy diamonds for themselves and to buy quality diamonds rather than the quarter or half carat that sells across the United States – the democratised diamond I would call this. It is these 'democratised diamonds' that have been crucial to the development of the Indian diamond trade.

Given the attention to transnational political economy it is important to understand the role of De Beers in the diamond trade and the impact of De Beers on global networks of trade and national governments. De Beers is the largest diamond mining company and the world's largest diamond producer. Through the Central Selling Organisation it sorts, values and sells approximately 80 per cent of the world's diamonds and it has done so since the 1930s when the cartel was formed. De Beers recently opened Venetia, a new mine in South Africa, and it has joint operations with the governments of Botswana and Namibia. It is a vast global enterprise which claims that through 'single channel marketing' it has been able to stabilise prices, balance supply and demand and stockpile rough diamonds against price falls. Sections of the diamond trade support these claims, others are less sanguine about De Beers, including sections of the Indian diamond trade.

Diamonds are released into the market by the five weekly 'sights' held in London at the CSO offices – cardboard boxes, rather like shoe boxes, containing rough diamonds, are offered to the sight holders. The sight holders are not in a position to negotiate around this rough, although they will make known to De Beers the type and quality of rough that they would prefer. The goods on offer to sight holders relate to their company and its assets but also location – large goods for Antwerp and smaller goods for Mumbai, for example. There are approximately 160 sight holders who are at the pinnacle of the diamond trade. To become a sight holder it is necessary to be financially very secure (De Beers does not like to take risks) and to have a proven record in the trade. Only those companies with large assets and who, on investigation, are shown to be *pukka* become sight holders. Initially these were companies based in London and Antwerp but in the 1960s the first Indian sight holder, B. Arun Kumar, joined the elite and to date there are thirty Indian sight holders. However, De Beers have until very recently shown very little interest in India. Nicky

Oppenheimer was the first of the Oppenheimers to visit India and that was in 1994.

Nicky Oppenheimer is the current chairman of De Beers, succeeding his father some five years ago, for, despite its status as a public, transnational company, De Beers is a family firm controlled and still owned by the Oppenheimers. The history of this South African Jewish family is a history of buy-outs, deals, etc., tied to the power of the Anglo-American Corporation and the business acumen of the Oppenheimer brothers, one of whom made money out of the First World War and set up the initial deal with Anglo-American banking (see Kanfer, 1993 for the details).

As the previous chairman of De Beers, Harry Oppenheimer, explained in relation to the monopoly position of the De Beers company:

> Whether this measure of control amounts to a monopoly I would not know, but if it does, it is certainly a monopoly of a most unusual kind. There is no one concerned with diamonds, whether as producer, dealer, cutter, jeweller or customer, who does not benefit from it. It protects not only the shareholders of diamond companies, but also the miners they employ and the communities that are dependent on their operations.

This seemingly idyllic consensus has, however, been ruptured in the last twenty years with challenges to De Beers from both the Russian diamond trade and the Argyle company mining diamonds in Australia. Argyle is actually part of the Rio Tinto Zinc group and thus part of an old rivalry between Anglo-American and RTZ. While these are the main players in a current drama that is currently being played in the Indian diamond trade, it is, I want to argue, pivotal to the reconstitution of the global scenario. Before I outline the recent history of these struggles between the main players let me briefly review the development of the Indian diamond sector.

Basically, diamond trading and processing came back to India in the 1960s in terms of volume but its antecedents lie earlier in the century and, as with the diamond trade more generally, this is a modern story — but not without its romance. Currently the diamond sector in India is dominated by a small number of large companies which are sight holders. These are Jain family firms and are interconnected through kinship tracing common origins to a small town in Gujarat called Palinpur. It is these Palinpuri Jains who are the big players in the trade and whose forefathers were the pioneers in relation to the very early development of trade in gems and jewels. Traditionally, Jains are traders in gems but the focus on diamonds, like banking, has developed in the modern era (see Carrithers and Humphrey, 1991 for an extended discussion of the Jains as a 'community'). Very briefly, and as far as I have been able to reconstruct this history, the Jains in Palinpur at the time of the Muslim princes were both 'diwan', functionaries of the princely state, and in a slightly different stratum also jewellers. The story is told that the functionaries became embroiled in a dispute between the prince and the British and that their integrity was threatened. Consequently, facing the British on one side and the power of the prince and growing numbers of Muslims, on the other, the Jains decided to move. One of their number started to trade in jewels, from the princes to Europe and, back from Europe to the princes, on an India-wide basis, setting up his headquarters in Mumbai. He encouraged Jains from Palinpur to join him in Mumbai and to learn what was becoming a developing gems trade which included, at the turn of the century and into the 1920s, the importance of Calcutta and Rangoon. Soon, these initial brothers had offices in Antwerp as well as Rangoon, Madras and Mumbai and in Antwerp they learned the diamond trade and started to sell cut and polished diamonds to the Nawabs for jewellery in India. Initially, the Mumbai outlet was Jhaveri bazaar and one of the brothers adopted this as his name. These brothers went on to create one of the largest diamond houses in India but one which has since had a major split between two brothers of the current generation. The links with Antwerp proved to be crucial for both the trade in diamonds and the expertise for processing diamonds which was brought to India in the 1960s. From this has grown a huge processing industry using the expertise of Indian cutters and polishers and the competitive labour rates at which the workers sell their skills. Equally important to the growth of the trade is kinship because the diamond trade has to be conducted in conditions of trust for which familiarity is essential. The close kinship links between the main purveyors and processors of diamonds enabled a very high level of control to be exercised over the trade. As many of the traders

confirmed it was not so much that it was Jains in the trade but that it
was a small number of interlinked families so the creditworthiness of
traders could be guaranteed. However, there was also the need for the
boundedness of the interlinked families offered by the community of
Jains. If an individual could not honour a deal then his father, uncle,
brother could be called upon to do so. Similarly, because the issue of
trust and thereby of risk was, and is, so crucial to diamond-dealing,
firms only expanded via family members, predominantly groups of
brothers and their sons. In this history is a story already familiar
through the Jewish trade in diamonds demonstrating the importance of
the articulations between economic factors, ethnicity and kinship
relations. This counters the abstracted model of economic relations and
confirms the embeddedness of economics in social relations. Clearly,
what was happening in India mirrored the power of De Beers, another
family firm with a powerful monopoly. What has happened since,
especially in the last twenty years, is a story of growth and fracture
straining the power of both these groups in the face of the phenomenal
growth of the diamond trade in India and world-wide.

Initially when the diamond trade in India expanded from the 1960s,
dealers in Mumbai looked to the hinterland for labour and locations
within a Gujarati network. The language of diamonds in India is
Gujarati alongside English, but there have been recent attempts to
introduce Hindi via publications from the Gem and Jewellery Council.
The Antwerp cutters and polishers came to Mumbai and Gujarat and
inducted skilled craftworkers into cutting and polishing. Surat was
close by and it was already growing because of the textile industry. It
provided an ideal location two to three hours from Mumbai with a
ready supply of competitive labour that could be policed through a
series of kinship connections. Gujaratis, from Saurashtra especially,
came into the diamond trade as production workers and some went
into dealing diamonds, but often it was a second generation who
headed for Mumbai and the sorting and valuing rooms. Trained in this
way by the large firms they moved into dealing. The whole sector grew
exponentially in twenty years until by the 1980s an estimated 800,000
to 1 million workers worked in processing diamonds, that is 95 per
cent of the cutters and polishers world-wide. Entrepreneurs could see
that the diamond trade was highly profitable, assisted by the tax break
given to all export sectors in India (exporters pay no tax on profits and

receive a licence to trade in diamonds as long as the goods can produce a 30 per cent value added). Thus, the diamond trade in India became the largest export earner in India if textiles and ready-made clothes are disaggregated. The export figures for 1995/6 of this sector are: gems and jewellery, $5447.61 million; cut and polished diamonds, $4661. 90 million. This accounts for 17.2 per cent of export earnings for India and is a new high. Equally important in these figures is the growth in the sale of rough diamonds which many of the original large firms now sell overseas, part of a strategy to promote India and Mumbai as a rough diamond trading centre.

From these figures it would appear that the diamond trade is booming whereas in fact the trade is in a slump which is seen by most of the large firms as a temporary downturn and by some of the smaller ones, who are barely surviving, as a serious threat. Generally, the Indian economy is in a downturn with many of the diamond dealers expecting a devaluation (currently 70R to the £ and 40R to the $). The stock market has slumped and manufacturing has slowed down, including in the diamond trade. This is very uneven but it has hit small firms and some have been bankrupted by a complex set of circumstances which I would argue is a form of restructuring which began in the 1980s.

Although the majority of diamonds in India still come via De Beers, for the last twenty years at least 20 per cent have been bought from Argyle and more recently, in unknown quantities, from Russia. Indian processing has become known for its work on small, low-quality diamonds, many of which come from the Australian Argyle mines. The cost of labour and the skills base in India was brought to these diamonds, which are exceptionally hard and difficult to process, as the basis for the 'democratised diamonds' of the USA which is the main export destination for cut and polished goods from India.

As with most of the world's diamonds, Argyle, like the Russian government, had an agreement with De Beers (to such an extent in the case of the Russians that De Beers was willing to put millions into the Gorbachev reforms when the Russian economy went into freefall). However, this very liberalisation has also created the conditions whereby the Russians no longer want an agreement with De Beers and discussions are ongoing while the amount of diamonds from Russia leaking into the market grows and grows. Argyle as a major volume producer – the largest rough diamond producer with 40 million carats per year (37 per cent of production) controls only 6 per cent of the global six billion dollar diamond market (backed by RTZ) because the diamonds are mainly for industrial use – had a five-year renewable agreement with De Beers which, after much haggling, bluffing and posturing, Argyle decided not to renew. Instead, Argyle went for 'betrayal' and has set up its own offices in Antwerp and in Mumbai, both to sell diamonds and offer technical advice, joint financing of diamond processing and a warm environment for Indian diamond traders. The initial impact on the Indian sector was panic and gloom (fearing prices would tumble) and in a highly charged meeting of the Gem and Jewellery Export Council one section wanted to halt all imports and production but this was not carried and the general view at the apex of the industry is 'wait and see'. However, for newer entrants into the trade, the Gujaratis from Saurashtra, the Argyle break with De Beers is seen as an opportunity and there are now 'Argyle traders' who deal only with Argyle direct. Some of these have been given financial support to start new state-of-the-art processing factories. De Beers claims that the Argyle move is no threat because it deals only in small, low-quality diamonds and because there is a suggestion that the Australian mining operation will be exhausted in five to ten years. However, with RTZ now prospecting in Canada and seeking to move into Russia the challenge to the cartel is very real. What makes it possible is the existence of the Indian industry. These changes are happening in the context of the over-production of diamonds, especially in relation to the saturation of the US market for smaller, low-quality goods. Instead, South-East Asia and China are the new target for volume sales. However, China too has a tradition of craftwork, and pre-empting the competition a number of the large Indian companies who regard China as the biggest threat to the Indian trade have already set up factories in the dollar zones.

However, there is a twist to the tale in so far as there is an over-production of diamonds which De Beers in the past have stockpiled in order to maintain prices through their control of the market. Without this prices are falling and especially the price of the Argyle diamonds. So Argyle may want to declare UDI but to optimise their profits they still need the power of De Beers to maintain the price of diamonds and the myth of diamonds as a scarce good, rare and valuable and, like the slogan, going to remain so.

What I would like to suggest is that we are witnessing the 'decentring of the diamond trade'. This is not only in relation to the Argyle/De Beers split within the context of over-production and massive leakage of diamonds from Russia, a number of other changes have also had a major impact on the trade, especially in India. Diamonds are traditionally exchanged for cash. A purchaser comes to view a quantity of rough in the sizes he requires and he can take this away with him and return in one or two days with cash for a sale or return the goods. Records of these transactions are made in small books, a simple accounting of goods for money. However, over the last couple of years credit has entered the trade which has allowed new people to enter but has also created major difficulties for small- and medium-size traders. The view from the field was that credit had been introduced by the US companies and that it had started as thirty days, which most people could cope with, and been extended up to a year. Thus, one of the large importers of polished diamonds in the States was using extended credit in this way and then the company collapsed with a domino effect on some of the Mumbai traders. One man I interviewed had ceased trading, having lost half a million dollars which his company could not carry. Instead, he has now set up a jewellery company which he considers a safer bet. Many of the traders underscored the deleterious effects of extended credit in an industry where profit margins are squeezed and so many companies are small and medium sized.

These processes of decentring – the Diamond Trading Corporation split with Argyle, over-production, expansion of the number of firms, falling prices, extended credit, saturation of the US market – contribute to a shift between the major controls that were possible over the Indian diamond trade and the current situation where another layer of activity has grown up beyond the trading and kinship links of the initial Jain families. For some of the traders I interviewed the real betrayal lies in the changing relations of the diamond trade from trust to mistrust fuelled by greed. This shift in the culture of the trade is also part of the modernity of which it is a part. Many of the older companies now have a third generation of sons and brothers and they emphasised that the trade was based on the integrity of the participants, 'an aristocratic business', 'for gentlemen'. As one man in Surat (who organises production for the huge Su Raj company) said, 'They do not undertstand that it is a royal trade.' Because trust was so crucial and because it is so difficult to police an expanded industry it has attracted adventurers and those in pursuit of quick bucks, which, of course, reproduces the diamond rushes of Kimberley a century earlier. Whether diamond production has ever been 'gentlemanly' and motivated by the integrity of *diamanteurs* rather than profits is, of course, debatable and part of the romantic rhetoric of the trade. But it was the case that the kinship links between a small number of families in the trade allowed trust to be backed by knowledge, surveillance and rough justice prevailed. The problems of policing workers in processing quite apart from selling in markets where participants are unknown quantities was an acknowledged difficulty. As one textile factory owner expressed it, 'I would never go into diamonds; too many headaches always having to watch the workers whereas in my factory the machines run and I can spend just two hours a day there.'

Trading diamonds

Diamonds are bought and sold in the creaking building known as Prasad Chambers in the old Opera area of Mumbai. The lifts work, sometimes carrying a stream of people (90 per cent men) up and down fifteen floors. On each floor there are security guards at the entrances to the firms. Behind these doors are often suites of rooms and offices for the large firms and very modest sorting and selling facilities for some of the newer entrants to the business. Consistent with the allure of diamonds and the notion of a gentlemanly pastime away from crude trade some of the large companies have very domesticated rooms into which clients are shown and where business is done. These rooms have large tables, lamps, ornaments, flowers and a plentiful supply of tea, coffee and cold drinks. This ambience, with its domestic atmosphere, contributes to a sense of intimacy between trader and client and confirms notions of trust and individuality which are reproduced in all the marketing literature, including materials from the Internet selling polished/cut diamonds. Diamond Brokers International, for example, addresses the purchaser through Internet pages which give information on cut, clarity, carats, shapes, etc., interspersed with comments like 'Whatever the shape, a well cut diamond is the work of a master

diamond cutter. When the cut is right the diamond gives more sparkle
… the look of a great gift and a good investment.' The pages end with:
'Don't rush into your diamond purchase. Take your time and evaluate
your choice carefully. It took thousands of years for nature to form
your diamond and the skill of a master diamond cutter to bring your
diamond to you. The time you now spend can bring you a lifetime of
pleasure.' On the ground this is reproduced in the elegant rooms of the
diamond factories of Amsterdam and the showrooms of Hatton
Garden.

The majority of diamonds traded globally are initially sold by De
Beers to the sight holders who come to London and view the rough
diamonds. This initial transaction is in cash and there is no credit for
syndicate goods. Dealers may now also purchase direct from Argyle in
Antwerp. Generally, there is no difference in the price which is still set
by De Beers. It is possible even that a buyer may pay slightly more from
Argyle because he can go direct and does not have to go via a sight
holder. Rough diamonds are usually sold in packets of 1,000 carats plus
and transported by courier or via British Airways to India. Indian
traders may also purchase from the Hindustan Trading Company but
they control only around 5 per cent of the total. The large sight holders
in India then sell on to dealers who sell on to smaller dealers down the
chain. Dealers acknowledged that they worked on a margin of 5–10
per cent, five or six times a year in relation to the sights and the
additional ongoing sales, but profit margins may be in excess of this.
There is currently no actual diamond bourse in Mumbai but it is being
built along with office space, shops, etc., in a new huge, government-
backed development near the airport. Clearly, diamond dealing,
especially for the smaller dealers, requires bank support for funds and
all the Indian banks are involved in this but large funds and the initial
financing comes from Antwerp which has been encouraged and
supported by De Beers. London-based diamond dealers complain that
British banks have been consistently unhelpful, which is part of the
reason that no one sets up in London but goes straight to Antwerp.
Although Jains are bankers and have been involved with money-lending
and banking throughout the century they did not have a role in the
diamond trade. Rough diamonds are sorted and sold in small packets
for processing and the 'official' expected return from packet to
processed diamonds is 1 to 10. If I buy rough for $50 I expect to sell it

when processed to jewellers for $500 but the profit may be much higher. Sorting is a constant process, when the rough is initially bought, then on request for particular sizes and qualities, and then again when it passes to the next dealer and then again when it goes for processing, and so on.

Engendering trust and risk

The domesticated ambience in which diamonds are sold generates the intimacy which is central to the trust relations which underpin the diamond trade. This domestication can also be viewed as feminised and allied with the end-consumers of diamonds, the majority of whom are women. The democratised diamond which has fuelled the diamond trade in India is made into jewellery gifted from men to women in the US seduced by the slogan 'a diamond is forever' and more recently, 'what can you buy with a month's salary that will last a lifetime?'. Engagement rings are signs of future intent and part of a modern era in which diamonds have been sold as signifying love and trust. But, behind this seemingly feminised world of diamonds bought and sold is actually a story bound to men and, like other forms of trade and money-making, it is bound to specific constructions of masculinity.

While colonial constructions of masculinities in India distinguished between the 'martial races' of the north and conceptions of masculinity bound to physical prowess (which produced the men drafted into the army and the police and sent around the world in this role) and had strong resonances with the Sikh account of the Khalsa, the alternative conception was bound to the feminised 'wily oriental', the Hindu man who was constructed as manipulative and untrustworthy (Westwood, 1995). These orientalist conceptions survive today but are part of a much more complex story. The power of money to define masculinity has become more important and in this the state of Gujarat had a head start due to the arrival of the trading era very early on and the East India Company. Surat, where diamonds are now processed, was the key commercial centre for India and produced wealthy merchants in the pre-colonial period. Some of these traders were Jains and the immense wealth of the community has continued. Money is given almost magical qualities and is related to all rituals in India while it provides status against caste background. The Jains, however, are recognised as a deeply religious community who, I want to argue, exercise a powerful hegemony in Gujarat and beyond on the pure and moral life. Jains observe strict dietary laws, fast, are involved in philanthropy and the building of elaborate temples which express their purity and godliness. Women especially are expected to observe fasts, and the process of renunciation is crucial to the Jain philosophy. Renunciation, of course, relies on the ability to possess material wealth that can be renounced as discussed by Laidlaw (1995) in his account of the gem dealers of Jaipur. The most recent and publicised renunciation was, indeed, a diamond dealer who reportedly threw diamonds to the crowd in Ahmedabad as he prepared to take up the ascetic life of a Jain 'monk'. This was a young man whose father is a well-known diamond dealer and who, very diplomatically, admitted his concern at his son's renunciation. The ascetic is certainly a variant of masculinity found throughout India but in Gujarat the power of trade and money has much greater currency.

Tambs-Lyche (1980) in an early account of Gujarati businessmen mentioned the articulation between business acumen and masculinity. It is not just that status accrues through wealth, rather that wealth is a measure of a clever businessman who knows the best tricks, the most lucrative deals and in order to have status and be validated as a man within *baniya*/trading communities the performance of masculinity requires the performance of trading acumen. Nowhere is this more evident than in the diamond trade where, like a broker or a commodity trader, the *diamanteur* requires skills in relation to risk and rough diamonds but also in relation to reading clients. Risk-taking is the mark of the enterprising self and a constituent of masculinity which is elaborated within the sites of the trading rooms and halls of the diamond world. This, like so many masculinities, is a masculinity validated by other men. Women are absent, on the whole, from Prasad chambers except as assistants and secretarial staff but they figure in the diamond story as emblems of success. Women display the effects of masculine prowess as traders in diamonds, especially at weddings, wearing exquisite jewellery and saris. This actually contrasts with the value Jains place on simplicity and their distaste for displays of conspicuous consumption favoured in other communities. The masculinity of risk-taking is opposed to the femininity of conservation and safety.

Diamonds are traded on the basis of trust but as Bloch and Parry (1989:4) note, 'once objects have become commodities in external trade they inevitably tend to become commodities within the community and to dissolve the bonds of personal dependence between its members'. The rhetoric of the diamond trade among Jains is a counter to this, reifying in effect the interpersonal bonds of kinship as the basis of trust in the business. Equally, the diamond trade is a global trade which is underpinned by these interpersonal, kinship relations that are now part of the Jain diaspora adding to the difficulties for trust relations and raising the importance of risk factors. However, commenting on Simmel, Bloch and Parry (1989: 5) note:

> While money erodes older solidarities, for Simmel it also promotes a wider and more diffuse sort of social integration. In the case of barter trust is confined to the parties directly concerned in the transaction; but monetary exchange extends the trust to an enormously expanded social universe.

Simmel raises, in effect, precisely the problem with which Mauss was concerned, the sphere of circulation and the embeddedness of circulation within social and cultural spheres. Latter-day anthropologists have read Mauss through Marx emphasising the triumvirate of production, consumption and distribution, recently extended in James Carrier's work (1995) to an analysis of the development of capitalist relations and the role of commodities within this.

In relation to the Indian international diamond trade the sphere of circulation invokes relations of trust which are central to the ways in which diamonds and money are moved around the world, from the dealers to the couriers. However, while trust is invoked the diamonds that travel from London to Mumbai on British Airways flights are also insured and have, on occasions, been 'misplaced' so that the risk factor has grown and damage limitation strategies have been reviewed. Risk management is expensive and is a booming sector of the capitalist economy. There is now a large and growing literature in sociology on risk following Beck's book *Risk Society*, taken up by Giddens and commented upon by Bauman. These writers are concerned with the growth of the middle classes and wealth more generally in the context of changing social relations which generate a sense of ontological insecurity among large sections of the population. The curiosity of this is that in the West people have never been safer in terms of health risks, war zones, etc. Nevertheless, the competitive quality of life and the freedoms that have been generated sustain feelings of immense insecurity and the middle classes are much exercised by the process of risk management in pursuit of sustaining lifestyles and positions. It is part of the reflexive self of late modernity and also, in another language, the enterprising self which manages life. Just as the diamond dealers calculate risk factors people more generally weigh up the odds and decide on a course of action. Economic models use rational choice theory to produce a series of outcomes through a set of models which are abstracted from the embeddedness of economic relations on which anthropology and sociology insist. One attempt to cross the divide was made by Granovetter (1985) who counters the notion of the abstracted market and seeks ways in which to insert interpersonal relations, especially those concerned with trust, into an economic model.

One of the main ways in which to manage risk is through keeping the business of diamond trading 'in the family' but this conceals the gendered quality of these relations. In a simplistic sense the major diamond houses are run by brothers who have inducted their sons into the trade. Keeping it in the family becomes a story of male affines and their offspring, the products of marriages within the diamond trade on the whole. However, I would argue that the story is more complex; trust is embodied but not a property of genes! Instead, trust is imbricated in the discourses and discursive construction of masculinity. Trust is honour and in the diamond trade, as in other trades, 'my word is my bond' applies but this has no meaning unless it is part of a conception of masculinity tied to valour, honour and *izzat*. Diamond dealers from the old school deal with each other as men of honour and celebrate their commitment to this. However, honour is backed by the network of kin relations in which it is embedded. Thus, as one trader commenting on the success of Jains in the industry noted, 'Well, partly we were the pioneers in the trade but more importantly among Jains you know which family you are dealing with and if a trader doesn't pay then you can contact his father or his uncle, and he does not want that to happen.' He does not want this to happen because his family will be shamed by him if he incurs bad debts or cheats. Thus in the realm of circulation it is honour that is constantly exchanged and reproduced against the backdrop of shame. Women are not part of this specific circulating system of honour. Daughters are not inducted into the trade, ostensibly because they marry out, but importantly because they cannot be bearers of honour in their own right within this system where honour is a constituent element of masculinity. Women as daughters, wives and mothers are bearers of male honour as they become signs of the wealth of a family through their dress and jewellery, and of purity through fasting and prayer. As the Indian diamond trade becomes increasingly globalised with diamond firms having offices in New York, Los Angeles, Bangkok and Shanghai the need to confirm trust and minimise risk is underlined. The answer lies in moving male family members around the globe but, as many of the older generation insisted, it is important for the men who travel to marry as soon as possible so that they will stay close to Jain values.

The complex of social and religious relations that construct the trust relations of the diamond trade were in many ways pre-figured in colonial India in relation to the Hindu merchants in Gujarat and in the south of India. David West Rudner's (1994) exploration of the articulation between caste and capitalism in relation to the mercantile elite of the Nakarattar business caste brings together the religious piety of this caste with the reproduction of social relations through religious and cultural institutions. This allowed a complex set of alliances which favoured commerce while reinforcing caste relations. The Jains, like the Ismailis, have been variously categorised as caste, ethnic or religious group and they actually use the permeability of this in relation to their own interests. It is very clear from the West Rudner study and my own research that there is no incompatibility between ritual and commerce and in the colonial period this was used to profit from colonial rule by the merchant bankers of the south. Central to this mobilisation of alliances was the understanding that people in the alliances could be trusted. In the same way that West Rudner suggests the use of caste as an umbrella concept, 'covering categories of people who are potential candidates for different kinds of practical and moral linkages', so the use of the term Jain is not unitary but may be conceived in this way. The symbolic capital generated through alliances was used in the pursuit of business strategies. In this chapter I have been trying to tease out the engendered/ethnicised qualities of this symbolic capital in the context of commercial enterprise.

Trust has long figured as a concern of sociologists, as discussed in Barbara Misztal's (1996) recent book which reconstructs discourses on trust from Durkheim, Simmel and Weber to more recent accounts by Giddens of the ways in which trust and risk are part of the increasing reflexivity of social life. Giddens emphasises the renewal of face-to-face forms of trust in late modernity alongside the more abstract forms that are constructed through symbolic systems and the role of experts. Misztal develops these notions and that of Luhman who understands trust only in relation to its functions. Taking the proposition, expressed again and again by the diamond dealers, that trust and the family are synonymous, it is clear that currently this couplet is under greater and greater scrutiny, especially in relation to the lives of children.

More generally, we can regard trust as habitus in which 'everyday routines, stable reputations and tacit memories' (Misztal, 1996: 102) contribute to a sense of social order and stability. For the diamond dealers there are acknowledged routines which are followed and which provide a stable framework for interactions within the trade. The contribution of stable reputations cannot be underestimated, dealers are tried and tested and known in the trade and this is symbolic capital which can, in relation to trading, become economic capital. Reputation must be worked on and over constantly and made visible, part of a performative power in relation to the wider space of diamond traders, within the Mumbai organisation, or the heady world of De Beers. Reputation is bound to honour and without it, within the world of Jain diamond traders, there is no business to be traded. Reputations are built over time and cherished in order to be secured for a new generation and the continuity of trade. For Jains this involves contributions to the building of temples, attendance at the temple, donations to good causes and a publicly honourable life. Diamond dealers in Antwerp, for example, where there are only 500 Jain families, raised millions of pounds for a new temple and Jain centre in a week and the whole community knew where donations originated. In this, the third aspect of the habitus of trust, 'tacit memories', is vitally important. The culture of the diamond trade among the Jains in Mumbai with its links to Antwerp and London knows its own history and places individuals and families in relation to this history. This is an oral history, carried from one generation to the next in which a story of migration, of success, and the ways in which people used their success for the benefit of others, is a constant reminder of the social responsibilities that lie within the community. Many Jains believe that their success is directly related to the fact that they help one another 'to go up', through contacts, money to start ventures and support along the way. This collective mode is seen as morally correct and contrasted with the competitive approach of the newcomers, the Gujaratis from Saurashtra, who have come into the trade in the last fifteen years, who suffer from boom and bust because they constantly try to outwit, undercut and cut down one another. This story is told without reference to the Jain dominance at the apex of the diamond trade and is, in part, a reflection on the attempts by these 'upstarts' to move in on a Jain sector of the economy. Misztal's account of trust as habitus is useful in analysing the place of trust in the Indian diamond trade. Equally, the notions from Beck (1992) and Giddens (1991) of the demystification of trust in relation to expert knowledge has a bearing upon the ways in which newer entrants to the trade see the diamond trade and their work. For them, the discourse of trust is part of the way in which the hegemony of the Jain traders is legitimised but, like the self-reflexive activist of Giddens' account, they too have acquired the knowledge and supplies via Argyle which allows them to enter the space of trading and in an often very masculinist way to pit their wits against the 'old boys club' of the Jain traders. They are the traders who are the entrepreneurial part of the democratised diamond of the current period.

Overseeing the daily interactions which support the account of trust among diamond traders is the power of De Beers who, like the dealers, make the same claims on sight holders and the sector more generally. De Beers can be trusted to work in the interests of the diamond trade overall as it claims and can back this claim by its reputation and its place in the collective memory of the trade.

Processing diamonds

From rough diamond to jewellery is a long process. Let me briefly move from sales to production processing and the products, cut and polished diamonds, that leave India for the world market. Only a very small part of this is actually jewellery and only a small part is consumed within India. The trained eyes of the dealers are able to assess rough for its ability to yield cut and polished diamonds with minimum waste and the highest potential. India processes a large volume of small, low-quality diamonds, some of which require considerable work to turn them into saleable items for jewellery. This processing may be done in-house by the large companies but even in-house means contracted and sub-contracted labour. One of the big five companies will at any one time be employing 10,000 workers, nearly all of them men, through contracting mechanisms. Diamond processing takes place in units from home production in the villages around Surat to the large modern factories of the export processing zone outside Mumbai. Surat has the largest concentration of factories and they range from the oldest to the newest technologies. One major problem for the diamond manufacturers is control of the diamonds and those in charge of the processing for the large companies are often relatives or trusted long-time manufacturers.

When the diamonds come into the factory they are sorted and then passed for further sorting and marking up for the initial cleaving. This first cut is crucial to a successful outcome. Marked-up diamonds will be cut in two ways, by traditional cleaving or, more common these days, by laser. Large companies will own lasers but smaller ones will send the diamonds out of house for laser cutting. Laser cutting is fast, works twenty-four hours and produces large quantities for volume production but not all rough diamonds are suitable and the loss on laser cutting tends to be higher so it is tied to volume production. Large, high-quality stones tend to be hand-cleaved in India. After initial cleaving the rough diamonds are then sorted again and the next process is bruting which gives a rough shape from which it is possible to cut the diamond. The brilliant is the most popular diamond shape, but a long piece of rough may be cut into a marquise shape or an oval and there are pear shapes, heart shapes, radiant and princess shapes – the latter require large, quality diamonds. The brilliant is cut in two sections above and below with a variety of different facets. There is a division of labour between workers who cut the top and those who cut the lower portion. Traditionally this work is done at low wheels using diamond dust and oil to facilitate the cuts but latterly this is both semi-automatic in which there are series of settings for cutting and completely automatic via computer technology much used in Israel and much less so in India. Polishing is the last stage of the process. At every stage diamonds are given out and returned to supervisors who watch over the workers against the possibility of theft and substitution of poorer quality diamonds. Workers in the large factories work at benches on semi-automatic machines. It is now said that it is possible to train cutters in a month for volume production.

One of the most newly built and modern factories I visited was a model factory with light rooms, plastic and silk flowers in an ornate mahal style building. Approximately 40 workers worked in sorting with a twenty-four-hour laser operated by one technician and additional rooms for cutting and polishing at semi-automatic machines. The factory was organised for volume production of up to 5,000 cut and polished diamonds produced each day for the American, Chinese, South-East Asian and Japanese markets. At the time of my visit it was producing 1,000–1,200 diamonds a day. This factory was new and the owner was justifiably proud of the building and the facilities for his workers among whom were a number of women in the sorting rooms. The workers were employed on a piece rate system which is reproduced throughout the industry at rates from 20R to 110R per day (1997) for experienced cutters working on larger diamonds. Working in factories at these kind of rates means that diamond workers are relatively well paid. Some are seasonal workers who have managed to save money for land and return to farming on a regular basis (Breman, 1996). At the other end of the scale is the cottage industry which may include children working in the home where rates are lower.

Diamond processing in India, because of the contracting and sub-contracting basis of the industry, employs, as I noted, in excess of 800,000 workers who it is estimated can be trained for diamond processing in a month. This contradicts the Diamond Institute where training takes at least nine months but does include design and jewellery elements as well. More importantly, it also contradicts the notion that the inherited skills of Indian craftsmen learned through the family over several generations is not reproducible elsewhere. In fact, the large diamond firms were clear that in terms of processing China was a major threat. Some of these firms have already opened factories in China even though the cost of processing is slightly higher. In part this is also a story of the cartel. The companies that have done this are De Beers sight holders and some of the smaller firms see this as part of a strategy by the Syndicate to wrest the control of diamond processing from India – time will tell. The main problem for the factories generally was control over the product with the possibility that at any one of a number of transactions the diamonds would be substituted or go missing. For this reason firms rely on people they know and test out new firms with small orders.

More generally there is a dilemma. The current over-production of diamonds and fall in prices has led to some workers being laid off and I did see factories that were not working with the contractors beginning to diversify into the production of specialist thread, textiles more generally, and so on. The contractors admitted that their own standard of living, which included private schooling at English-medium schools, cars and well-furnished apartments, was fairly secure but for the workers there was the additional threat of new technology. Factories in Israel are capital intensive and some diamond firms saw this as the way forward, conscious that employment in the industry was a vital resource for the region as well as the individual workers. For the large companies the dilemma could currently be solved by a division of labour with 'high tech' factories as new ventures but the need for labour maintained in relation to the lower quality stones. They could have it all ways for the moment. But the Diamond Institute was planning a 'high tech' future for diamonds in India as the way in which the sector would be maintained against competition from elsewhere. The big firms also engage in diversification from major shares in the new private airlines to huge 'state of the art' hospitals for the growing private health market which attracts overseas clients as well as the home market. Construction, property and the stock market have all benefited from the diamond boom and the diamond magnates have gleaned profits moving from one sector to the next. One thing they are all clear about is that no one wants a political career – too tarnished and 'it's better to use politicians than become part of that game'.

Diamonds are forever?

The diamond trade boomed in India through the 1970s and the 1980s but in the late 1990s there was an unprecedented downturn and sense of insecurity among commentators, merchants and processors. It was not uniform; newcomers to the business are full of optimism, like the new owner of the model factory in Surat who anticipates volume production and large profits. Equally, the uncertainties are being absorbed within the largest companies who have a global network, secure finance and a strategy of diversification. These leading figures caution against panic and want to 'wait and see' for the next twist in the diamonds story. These huge companies can, of course, be publicly philosophical while privately they are busy developing alternatives and working new trajectories for the trade in China and elsewhere. The large companies exercise a controlling interest in the diamond sector in India, are sight holders and thereby tied to De Beers trajectories. These companies are a secure, small group of Palinpur Jains who initially pioneered the trade in diamonds and who now run factories, make jewellery, export it around the world and are encouraging the home market as well.

But for the smaller companies these are uncertain times and on a much smaller scale some have also opted for jewellery manufacture against the trade in diamonds. Yet, as I suggested, newer entrants are full of confidence and this is, in part, developed from the ways in which the trade has opened up to them. New companies can go directly to Argyle for diamonds, organise production and seek out markets against the constraints of the previous era. It may be risky but there are still steady and sometimes large profits to be made. Officially working on 5–10 per cent margins over a large number of transactions can produce high levels of profit.

More generally, it is suggested by the large companies that India needs to move into rough diamonds and become a much larger player in this field. In part the success of this strategy relates to the ongoing relations between De Beers and Argyle and the role of the Russians. India's entry into the rough trade would be part of the restructuring of the global diamond market and would add to the pressure on De Beers and relaxation of the monopoly. De Beers will not give up the cartel easily – it has been threatened before and De Beers with its phenomenal wealth and inter-governmental links has manoeuvred itself sufficiently to stay in place at the apex of the whole trade, exercising a high level of control over the global supply of rough diamonds and continuing to pay high dividends to shareholders. However, the romance of diamonds is beginning to unravel, not only in the splits from De Beers but also in the growth of the Indian sector and the entry of China and South-East Asia as players. However, the Indian merchants are already in the game and are potentially some of the makers of the rules in the next decades.

Equally important for the romance is the claim to honesty and integrity which, too, has begun to unravel in the face of expansion. The arrival of a new generation of adventurers who expressly challenge the dominance of the 'old boys', as they call the large Jain companies in India, is another challenge. Newcomers are matched by the arrival of new technology which, as always in India, is a contradictory story. New technologies promote volume production but are capital intensive against the low cost of labour and the importance of employment. It is also clear that the claim for the skills of the Indian workforce overall has been challenged by the notion that a cutter can be trained in a month. Instead, one strategy is to maintain a superior and highly trained elite of diamond cutters against the volume production. This will promote India as a cutting centre on an equal footing with Antwerp and Israel producing quality goods – basically going up-market, which some of the older, smaller firms have successfully achieved using traditional skills for a specific market. On the other hand there is a new marketing strategy for the 'democratised diamond', one might want to suggest that an MTV generation, especially young men, be sold the diamond stud – one for each ear – as the fashion statement for the new century.

The modern diamond trade, from De Beers to the cutters and polishers in Surat, is a clear example of transnationalism. The trade demonstrates the importance of the articulation between global and familial concerns, from De Beers the family to the wealthy Jains at the apex of the Indian diamond trade. Migration is a central part of the story, one which is further explored in the second part of this book. It is clear that both goods and people move as part of the global market and the ways in which goods and people are intertwined have been explored in this chapter through elaboration of familial strategies in which trust and risk play a major part. These themes are further explored in Chapter 7, 'Men, women and business'.

Acknowledgements

The research that forms the basis of this chapter would not have been possible without the generous and patient assistance of members of the Jain community in Mumbai and so many diamond dealers in Mumbai, Surat, Antwerp and London, especially the Mehta family, Dr Shah and Dr Jhavieri. Warmest thanks to everyone. The project is grateful for assistance from the Dr N. K. Shah Foundation and the University of Leicester. Thanks also to Nick Jewson with whom the research began.

Notes

The Jains currently constitute less than 1 per cent of the population of India but exercise enormous influence economically and culturally in relation to Hindu India. The collectivity is divided by caste, doctrinal debates and interpretations of religious practice in everyday life. Jain religious beliefs and practices share elements with Hinduism, like a commitment to the doctrine of *karma*, while claiming that the religion is older and emphasising Buddhist asceticism. Jains do not celebrate festivals but they do invest in lavish temples. Central to Jain religious beliefs is the doctrine of *ahimsa* (non-violence), which translates into a strict vegetarian dietary code, employment beyond agriculture, mining and in commerce, banking and certain professions. Renunciation of the everyday world is highly valued and there are both men and women ascetics often termed 'monks' and 'nuns' in English which is a poor representation but does emphasise the commitment to a spiritual life. It is part of the commonsense understanding that Jains have prospered due to their asceticism and piety but, as this chapter suggests, Jains in the diamond trade foreground the social relations of Jain networks as more important.

Making connections
Transnationals, nation and migration

Ruptures

In the first part of the book we have looked at the notion of ruptures in relation to the nation-state and processes of globalisation. In particular we have been concerned to examine the formations and reproduction of the nation-state in Latin America, demonstrating the ways in which nations are not homogenous nor finished products but are constantly being worked on and over to secure their existence. In the next chapter we look at ruptures in a slightly different way. We ask whether the shifts in the ways in which migration has been theorised over time constitute a number of ruptures in our theoretical understanding of migration.

In addition the suggestion that the global and the local are two separated worlds is challenged in this chapter. The thrust of the globalisation thesis has often suggested that we live in postnational times whereas, as this chapter argues, on the contrary, ours is a deeply national time in which affluent nation-states grow ever more concerned with their borders and mechanisms for keeping people within and without. In other words: 'the question of "need" is no longer about them and theirs, it's about us and ours' (Fonseca in the *Guardian*, 24 March 2000). This is the language of property and propriety which sits uneasily with an account of mobility and the freedom of movement suggested in political rhetoric.

The politics of belonging

In the first part of the book we have concentrated attention upon the ways in which the nation forms a focus for a sense of belonging and addressed the means by which people move their sense of national identity around the globe. Thus, Anderson's conception of political love as a way of understanding the investments that people have in the national project is examined once again in relation to the claim that we now live in postnational times. It is clear from the analysis that the processes of identification are often contingent and fleeting, expressed in relation to the national football team or forms of popular culture. But this suggestion that all is transitory is re-examined in relation to the growth of Latino/a cultures in the US. North and South America are a mirror dance in which the impact of the North has been keenly felt in the South but in which latterly the South has moved North to join the diasporic cities of the US. This chapter has sought ways in which to understand the impact of this mobility on North American urban cultures and to describe and explain the cartography of belonging that is emerging within Latino/a cultures. The ways in which people claim the spaces of the city as their own and the changing sense of identity that accompanies these shifts is central to this process. In part, this is expressed through popular culture and the huge boom in Latino/a music, food and dance styles that mark the current phase in the US.

In the second part of the book the notion of home is examined in relation to migration and the politics of belonging in two main ways. First, faced with the theoretical impasse that we allude to in Chapter 5, both economists and sociologists began in the 1980s to focus their interest on the 'household' as a central institution in the migratory project. We look critically at how this interest in the household reflected (and in much of the literature continues to reflect) a traditional view of gender roles. Women in these households are viewed in a passive way either as followers of men or more dependable remittance senders than male household members. Rather we want to suggest an alternative view where women's agency is expressed in independent decision-making and a recognition that migration may be the best way of bringing a better life to *themselves as well as* to their families. Secondly, we want to show through an analysis of the campaign for justice by migrant domestic workers in London that these individual transformatory projects are also capable of becoming collective transformatory projects. For all of these workers the politics of belonging is a hugely complicated affair, not just in a legal sense as they strive to regularise their immigration status, but in an emotional sense as well, where 'home' has become stretched over time and space.

Economic ethnoscapes

While the earlier chapters have drawn upon the cultural and imaginary world of nations and belonging our final theme addresses the economic moment but not in either a foundational or an isolated way. In Chapters 4 and 7 the analysis weaves its way around and through the economic and cultural moments, avoiding a cultural essentialism as securely as it avoids economic determinism. In both chapters our concern is with the embeddedness of economic relations in ethnic and familial processes. These chapters return to the importance of riches and wealth amongst transnational elites but re-emphasise the point that such elites have been operating in such a way since the thirteenth century and that a global notion of trade has not been invented with the Internet.

Part II

Chapter 5

Ruptures

Migration and globalisation: looking back and looking forward

Annie Phizacklea

Over the last twenty-five years the economies of the so-called advanced industrial countries have undergone massive restructuring and change, changes which not only tore the heart out of the traditional centres of labour-intensive and extractive industries in Western economies but virtually decimated the traditional labour movement. We have witnessed the continuing rise of women's paid employment and a continuing decline in full-time male jobs leading many to talk of 'the feminisation of the labour force' (Reskin and Padavic, 1994). This phrase not only refers to the increased numbers of women in paid employment but (aided by the deregulation of national economies) also to a deterioration in the terms upon which both men and women are employed in the pursuit of 'flexibility' in the workforce. Fewer and fewer employees can now expect the kind of permanency, security or employment protection that characterised so much of male employment twenty-five years ago.

As the old political and economic divisions between the 'communist' East and the West collapsed, we witnessed the further weakening or demise of traditional parties of the Left and the ascendance of the market economy at a global level. We are frequently reminded that we apparently live in a world where the process of globalisation has reached a point where national boundaries, economies and cultures are of little importance. We cannot ignore the significance of the activities and investment decisions of transnational corporations, nor the elimination of national barriers to trade and investment, nor the rapid developments in information and communication technologies which have literally transformed the ordering of space and time in our lives.

But all of these changes led to social dislocation on a massive scale, in the first four years after the collapse of the Soviet Union an estimated nine million people had been temporarily or permanently displaced within the geographical space that constituted the former Soviet Union. Even greater numbers are apparently on the move in Southern China alone, due to the incredibly rapid rate of industrialisation in that part of the country (Huang, 1999). Even before the Kosovan war an estimated five million people had been displaced in the ethnically based war-torn Balkans (UNECE, 1995). Whether migrants are labelled 'economic' or 'political', 'voluntary' or 'forced', they must all eventually accommodate themselves to the social and economic challenges that migration brings with it.

Set against the political transformations, the massive internationalisation of capital and the subsequent social dislocation, individual nation-states have become increasingly restrictive about the movement of people transnationally. Capital may want a global labour force, but nation-states are often reluctant to see that happen. What has been labelled 'Fortress Europe' is a prime example, where the mobility of citizens of member states is encouraged, but the movement of anyone else is closely monitored or completely restricted. Apart from the highly qualified it has been virtually impossible for so-called 'economic' or labour migrants to enter the European Union and work legally for the last twenty-five years. Stuart Hall writing as the single European market was officially launched had this to say:

> As Europe consolidates and converges, so a similar exercise in boundary maintenance is in progress with respect to its Third World 'Others'. ... Political refugees deserve refuge in enlightened Europe, home of liberty. Usually they are few in number, and it is often hard to prove conclusively that they are in direct danger from some oppressive or tyrannical regimes of the kind which poverty and indebtedness breeds – which allows a reasonable proportion to be bundled unceremoniously back to the waiting arms of the local police.
>
> Economic migrants, on the other hand, are simply unwitting casualties of the 'normal' processes of market forces as they operate at the periphery. Europe, whose banking arrangements have destroyed subsistence agriculture and whose new Gatt arrange-

ments will price them out of the commodity markets, owes them nothing … suddenly, European prosperity is a strictly European affair designed exclusively for what every self-respecting Euro-politician is calling 'our populations'.

(Hall, 1992: 2)

Little did Hall realise that the tendencies evident in 1992 would become an even more elaborate system of fortification where European states have extended restrictive immigration policies to cover asylum seekers too. Even though this policy flies in the face of international understandings which suggest that asylum seekers should be assessed differently to other types of migrants, current policy is designed to prevent the arrival of asylum seekers in the first place. Koser argues: 'These include the growing list of countries from which visas are demanded; the promotion of "safe" havens; the requirement that asylum seekers submit their applications at a consulate or embassy in their country of origin; and carrier sanctions' (Koser, 1997: 187). In addition asylum seekers can be returned to those countries deemed as 'safe' and through which it can be proved they have travelled.

The frequent use by politicians of the construct 'genuine–phoney' when referring to asylum seekers and refugees and its reporting by newspapers has certain outcomes:

the frequency of use over time of these expressions by newspapers is potentially more significant in influencing public opinion than whether articles are in themselves sympathetic to refugees or critical of politicians for denigrating them.

(Kaye, 1997: 179)

For the last thirty years in Europe we have witnessed how successfully right-wing politicians shift the terms of debate around immigration to the right. This results in a situation where member states may be quick to agree on co-operation between police authorities and interior ministries to enforce increasingly restrictionist policies but fail to demonstrate any commitment to tackling racial discrimination and violence on a union-wide basis (Phizacklea, 1994).

Within this context we have seen all European countries reducing the access of applicants for asylum to welfare and to work, competing to see how unattractive they can make themselves to would-be applicants. In the Cold War years the US and Western European countries welcomed Soviets who were 'fleeing from communism', but it welcomes them no longer unless they have demonstrable 'use value'. Nor does Europe want to know about the hundreds of thousands of 'transit' migrants from countries such as Afghanistan, Iraq and Somalia who flowed into Russia and other post-Soviet states after they hastily adopted the 1951 Geneva Convention on Refugees in 1992. Co-dagnone argues that this has resulted in a situation where:

> Given the post-Soviet states' lack of experience and financial resources to deal with this situation, these migrants, once they have bounced off the closed walls of 'Fortress Europe', find them-selves in shaky camps in very poor living conditions.
>
> (Condagnone, 1997: 44)

The scale and pace of economic and political change world-wide has changed the nature of migration, twenty-five years ago we were absorbed with the implications of labour migration and the study of migration reflected this. Now we are preoccupied with, on the one hand, the multiculturalism that those labour migrations brought with them and the hybrid cultures that they represent and, on the other hand, the flows of refugees, asylum seekers and undocumented migrants that political upheaval and restrictionist immigration policies have created. We then have to ask, have these changes been reflected in a reconceptualisation of the way in which we theorise and analyse those changes? To what extent have they been reflected in theoretical ruptures? We want to argue that there are certain strands of theoretical change, but also stasis. The latter reflects the ways in which migration theory fell into a kind of impasse between the neo-classical economic accounts of the 1960s and the neo-Marxist political economy accounts of the 1970s. Both were driven by the need to explain labour migration. One way out of the impasse was simply to focus on those institutions which link the individual migrant with macro-structural factors, institutions such as the household and social networks (Boyd, 1989). An alternative approach was to think of migration as a system which brought these three levels of analysis together (for instance Fawcett and Arnold, 1987). Others went one step further in arguing that it was possible to produce paradigms capable of explaining both economic or other forms of voluntary migration as well as 'forced' migrations, such as refugee flows (Richmond, 1988). These shifts in theory hardly constitute a 'rupture', rather a succession of minor fractures that did not seem to heal up very well.

The second 'rupture' was disciplinary or the failure to produce truly interdisciplinary accounts of migration and settlement. This has led to a situation where the study of 'ethnic' and often 'race' relations as well have peeled off from the study of migration, which in turn has largely ignored important developments in women's studies, feminist theory and cultural studies. We look a little more closely at this in the next chapter. In what follows here, we map out some of these tendencies and how we might start to draw them together. To a certain extent it is a story about how the meta-narratives such as Marxism came under attack as a way of explaining the world, how the centrality and relevance of class analysis in the face of persisting gendered and racialised inequalities came into question. Terms such as 'women' or 'black' were deconstructed to reveal the diversity of experience that lay within them. Migratory flows are diverse, they incorporate men, women and children of different nationalities and linguistic, ethnic and religious affiliations. Some have documents, some have not. Some migrate in search of work, others are fleeing persecution, some are highly skilled professionals, some have limited skills. The diversity is endless, even before we begin to compare the legal position, and therefore the potential for maximising human capital, between migrants as non-citizens and citizens in the migration setting. What is important is that we do not allow the difference and diversity to obscure the very real material inequalities and positionings which that diversity represents.

Nearly twenty years ago a group of eight feminist academics came together to share their interest in the issue of women, migration and work, the outcome being an edited volume called *One Way Ticket: Migration and Female Labour* (Phizacklea, 1983). Looking back on that work it is interesting to see the range of conceptualisations that each of us brought to what was then a new area of academic interest. In our group discussions we agreed that variety was a strength, not a weakness, but agreed 'to adopt the conceptualisation of migrant women workers as the bearers of a triple burden – as women, as migrants and as workers' (Phizacklea, 1983: 11). One of the ways in which that conceptualisation was presented was a straightforward socialist feminist 'line', reasonably typical of the late 1970s and early 1980s. It ran as follows:

> The vast majority of migrant women from the European periphery and the Third World can be described as working class, by virtue of the fact that they sell their labour power for a wage and are predominantly located in semi- and unskilled manual jobs. Nevertheless their objective position within that class is determined by their specific position within economic, politico-legal and ideological relations, factors which underpin complex racial and sexual divisions within the working class ... do all such women occupy the same objective position within the class structure, or put differently, are they part of the same racially and sexually categorised fraction of the working class?
>
> (Phizacklea, 1983: 95)

Thus while the class analysis was complicated by the admission that racialised and gendered relations, discourses and practices played a part, it was capitalist relations that remained central to the analysis:

> migrant labour, having been 'produced' by the demand for labour in socially undesirable and low-wage sectors of the economy, is confined to those sectors, often by specific policies and practices which are partially justified by the ascription of inferior characteristics, the consequence then being viewed as vindication of the ideology.
>
> (ibid.)

The subsequent analysis of labour market data for migrant women in Britain, France and Germany in the early 1980s led to the conclusion that indeed their position warranted the description of 'a sexually and racially categorised class fraction' (Phizacklea, 1983: 109). Women working in the so-called 'ethnic economy' were analysed in terms of their 'role in the process of class formation within migrant populations'.

This preoccupation with establishing the 'objective position of migrant women in the class structure' was tempered by a recognition of the role of their agency, but as 'active protagonists in class struggle' (ibid.:110). Having considered a number of industrial disputes, the analysis goes on to argue that

> Migrant women have repeatedly demonstrated their resistance to the exploitation they experience in the workplace and yet to date they have been marginalised by the very institutions of the labour movement which supposedly exist to protect and defend their interests as wage-labourers. Self-organisation and activity may have been forced on migrant women in the workplace but self-organisation is in itself a prerequisite for migrant women's struggle against their triple oppression. ... Many of the most pressing issues for migrant women are not over wages or degrading working conditions, they relate to basic human rights; the right to stay in the country, to be joined by their children, to have a decent place to live, to be free of racist harassment and violence. There is increasing evidence that migrant women are setting up their own organisations through which they can speak for themselves and articulate demands specific to their fractionalised class position.
>
> (Phizacklea, 1983: 111)

While such an analysis may not have been completely guilty of what Monica Boyd describes as 'an oversocialised view in which people were passive agents in the migratory process, projected through time and space by social forces' (Boyd, 1989:641), nevertheless what we do see is the reduction of human agency to the interests of a collective agency – the global 'working class'.

The analysis was typical of a larger body of work informed by Marxist political economy and which drew heavily on dependency theory and world systems theory. Authors such as Meillassoux argued, for instance, that the maintenance of racism was essential 'for the over exploitation of the so-called under-developed peoples' and to keep the latter in a constant state of fear (Meillassoux, 1981:121). The work of Castles and Kosack (1973), Castells (1975), Nikolinakos (1975) and Buroway (1980) was all cast within this political economy of migration model. When we reread these accounts they smack of an economic determinism which has become distinctly unfashionable in sociological circles, particularly in their preoccupation with the economy and class analysis.

However, even if the mode of conceptualisation may now seem mechanical and economistic it drew attention to a number of factors which are as relevant to contemporary analyses as they were twenty years ago. It emphasised that women as well as men may migrate in search of work and that they do not simply 'follow' men. It endeavoured to produce an account which both recognised migrant women as agents, individual and collective, and their being subject to external constraint. In the latter case it was argued that colonialism and the trade and investment practices of post-colonialism have produced vast regional inequalities on a global scale. In the short to medium term economic development does not reduce the pressure on individuals to migrate in search of a livelihood, on the contrary it actually increases that pressure because of the economic and social dislocation that accompanies the development process. The mechanisation of agriculture and the industrialisation process itself are not gender neutral in their impact. For instance, deprived of traditional subsistence and cash-generating activities on and around the land it is often women who become a relative surplus population in the poorer developing countries of the world. Even though from the late 1960s these same countries became the favoured sites for low-wage manufacturing production in world market factories set up by transnational companies the supply of women workers outstrips available employment. Migration provides an economic escape route (Phizacklea, 1983). But it provides a social escape route as well. Research on Irish and Yugoslav women migrants indicates that migration was not always an enforced response to economic hardship, but also a calculated move on the part of individual gendered actors who could see that migration also served as an escape route from a society where patriarchy was an institutionalised and repressive force (Morokvasic, 1983 and Gray, 1996). Finally, 'external constraint' or 'structural' factors were never simply cast in economic terms in these early accounts. The existence of state masculinism through the workings of immigration legislation and the application of immigration rules was well recognised.

While some of the more overt sexual discrimination enshrined in immigration law has subsequently been successfully challenged, in the case of the UK this was done through 'levelling down': men's rights were simply reduced to those of women's. In other ways state masculinism continues to work in such a way that certain groups, for instance, women from South Asia, are disadvantaged. The existence of the 'primary purpose rule' means that many women from South Asia have not been permitted to live with their husbands in the UK. As Bhabha and Shutter have argued: 'The assumption is that Asian men following their wives to Britain must have had immigration as their primary purpose in marriage. Assumptions about family relationships and the primacy of male work and male decision-making still influence policy and the exercise of discretion' (Bhabha and Shutter, 1994:2). Werner Menski argues that the law is intentionally ambiguous, allowing entry clearance officers a huge realm of discretion (Menski, 1999: 82). Appeals statistics indicate that the vast majority of male spouses refused entry are from the Indian sub-continent (Southall Black Sisters, n.d.: 16). Spouses, male or female, who do manage to enter on the basis of marriage are then obliged to stay within the marriage for one year before they are given indefinite leave to remain. During this period they are not eligible to receive welfare benefits. While the rule applies to both men and women, evidence suggests that it is women and children who are most affected by it and as a result can be trapped in violent and abusive relationships with a stark choice: put up with the abuse or be deported (ibid.: 28). A failed marriage is a source of shame for many women whatever their ethnic background, but for many Asian women (and not just from the Indian sub-continent) it can mean ostracism from family and community alike. In the next chapter we shall see how this dilemma can be an incentive for women to migrate initially (a factor noted by Mirjana Morokvasic more than twenty years ago in her research with Yugoslav women migrants) but to be caught in an unsatisfactory marriage in the migration setting, in the circumstances described above, it can mean real entrapment.

Thus when we talk about 'structural' or 'external' constraint we are not simply talking about poverty, or the occupational crowding of migrant women into poorly paid, 'feminised' jobs, we may also be talking about insurmountable legal obstacles which determine individual lives.

What we are saying therefore is that the structural constraints that limit individual decisions about migration are no less important today than they were twenty-odd years ago. In fact, as we have seen they are even more clear cut. The processes of globalisation may have benefited many in those parts of the world that were already affluent, but the gap in living standards between these countries and regions and the developing world is now even greater. As that gap has widened so has the determination of the affluent world to keep out the ragged global army of the dispossessed by ever more restrictive immigration controls. If the structuralist political economy accounts of migration erred in the direction of an 'oversocialised' view of migration then they proved an antidote to misleading and outdated neo-classical economic accounts which saw the migrant as a rational decision-maker setting off with his or her suitcase to the country best suited to the maximisation of their human capital.

The work of Todaro is representative of the neo-classical economic approach (Todaro, 1969 and 1976) and can be summed up as a prediction that the volume of transnational migration is significantly related to the real or expected international earnings gap (Massey *et al.*, 1993: 455). Thus at a macro level we are analysing a situation where the 'push' factors determining outward migration are low wages and living standards, probably structural unemployment. While the 'pull' factors are migration destinations which offer employment and higher wages. At a micro level the model assumes that individuals make rational choices about migration, that they weigh up the costs and benefits and will move to the destination which maximises the net return on migration. Part of this equation will be individual human capital characteristics, such as education and training, that will increase the individual's likelihood of gaining employment or higher wages in the migration setting (Borjas, 1990).

While such assumptions have been heavily critiqued, they have influenced the position on migration adopted by a number of developing countries, the Philippines being a prime example. In the latter case, migration has long been positively encouraged to relieve internal poverty and to service foreign debt. By law migrant workers must remit between 30 and 70 per cent of their earnings and in 1992 the government collected $9.6 million in passport fees alone (Chant and McIlwaine, 1995: 33). Skeldon reports that in 1996, remittances (that went through official channels) to the Philippines from just two destinations, Hong Kong and Singapore (where the vast majority of remittance senders are women domestic servants), were over US$250,000 (Skeldon, 1999: 20). As we shall see in the next chapter, women are very careful about who the money goes to, usually someone they trust completely and with whom they will have agreed how the money will be spent, the most often stated reason being for their children's or siblings' education.

Remittances do constitute an important economic contribution to governments and families alike, but increasingly migrants are saddled with debts to intermediaries (such as employment agencies, traffickers, etc.) which means prolonged absence and vulnerability in the migration setting.

As the human capital part of the equation would predict it is not the least educated and trained that migrate, quite the reverse (see Foner, 1977 for Jamaican migration) but if individuals believe this will improve the probability of their gaining employment commensurate with their qualifications then they are likely to be disappointed. There is in fact considerable evidence to show underemployment of migrants from poor countries and few opportunities to acquire new skills or further education in the migration setting. For instance, a study of Filipina domestic workers carried out in Rome and Milan in 1991 indicated that half of the 101 women interviewed had college educations and complained bitterly about the obstacles to their gaining better employment or qualifications in the migration setting (LIFE, 1991). Research carried out in Spain in 1996 indicated that Filipina women were the preferred nationality group as maids in families with children precisely because they could teach the children English. Their bilingual skills were taken for granted and there was no additional financial reward for the provision of this specialised skill (Anderson, 2000).

Thus whether the account is pitched at the macro or micro level we can see that neo-classical economic accounts provide a limited understanding of transnational population movements. Individual, 'rational' choices must be analysed within the context of external constraint such as immigration policies which are not capable of manipulation by individuals. Nevertheless these accounts are important in stressing the role of agency and while individuals may act on very imperfect information as regards the migratory decision, those decisions are not wholly shaped by external constraint.

While these early accounts are ungendered it is possible to indicate how the argument would run if one adopted this model in relation to women's migration. Basically the argument would run that faced with poverty and unemployment women in poor countries would view access to low-paid work through migration 'as better than nothing'. Not only would migration offer the possibility of providing access to a wage and therefore to remittances but this would have an 'emancipatory' potential for women, strengthening their economic and social position and power within households.

However flawed the neo-classical economic accounts were we can now see that there was a tendency, as Boyd has argued, to replace 'an undersocialised view of migration in which all action reflected individual wishes and preferences' with an oversocialised structural alternative (Boyd, 1989: 641). Twenty years on there is a recognition that if we want to explain why it is that individuals migrate we need to combine analyses of structural and external factors with situational, micro-level understandings and we would add that this has to be done in a gendered way. It is vital that any account of migration emphasises the role of individuals as active protagonists in the process. It is so often assumed that women merely follow men in the migratory process, that they are reactive rather than proactive. This is not the case. Agency and not just structure must be at the heart of those accounts if we are to avoid the tendency to treat migrant women as victims, as passive agents tossed around the world at the beck and call of transnational capital. Rather they will focus on women's role as active decision-makers, on their economic contribution and their efforts to improve their own and their families' standard of living. They also provide space for analysing individual and collective transformatory practices. As Kamala Kempadoo has argued: 'By underlining agency, resistances to, and contestation of, oppressive and exploitative structures are uncovered and the visions and ideologies inscribed in women's practices made visible' (Kempadoo, 1998: 9). In the next chapter we explore some aspects of contemporary migration within such a framework.

Two alternative ways of conceptualising migration emerged during the 1980s and 1990s. One was to look at migration as a system, stressing the historical and social linkages that usually exist between sending and receiving societies (Fawcett and Arnold, 1987). Thus at the macro level we would look at factors such as colonial ties or trading links and we would also look at the informal social networks which link migrants and non-migrants across time and space. For instance, if we look at Jamaican migration to the UK in the 1950s we can see how these linkages operate at both a macro and a micro level. Up until the introduction of restrictive legislation in the early 1950s the United States had been the favoured destination for Jamaican migrants driven out by the underdevelopment of a colonial economy with one use, the production of sugar cane. As British interest in sugar cane declined so did the island's economic and social condition. Migration, first to help build the Panama canal and then later to the United States, provided an escape route from unemployment (Foner, 1977: 124). Restrictions on entry to the US coincided with a demand for labour in the United Kingdom. Until the Commonwealth Immigrants Act of 1962, citizens of the Commonwealth were free to enter and to work in Britain. The initial wave of migrants who arrived in Britain from Jamaica were skilled and semi-skilled workers. Despite racialised discrimination they found jobs and somewhere to live and wrote home telling friends and family of job opportunities. Thus what is called a 'chain migration' began with social networks facilitating further migration to Britain. The existence of those networks meant that money could be sent to help others migrate as well as providing information on jobs and housing. In this way we can see how migration is never a haphazard or spontaneous process. In fact there is clear evidence that in the Jamaican case migration was 'self-regulating' up until the imposition of restrictions in 1962; men and women would arrive when there were job vacancies and when there were few vacancies, migration would fall off in terms of numbers entering (Peach, 1968). Thus migration systems theory indicates the importance of looking at political, economic and social linkages at both the macro and micro level.

In the next chapter we pay more attention to the intermediaries that facilitate migration from the household to the proliferation of employment agencies and brokers that have institutionalised the process of migration.

One theory?

A frequent criticism of the theorisation that we have looked at so far is that whatever their strengths and weaknesses they were developed to explain labour migration and have little explanatory power in helping us analyse the 'forced' or 'involuntary' migrations of refugees and asylum seekers. The work of Anthony Richmond is important here in both questioning the distinction between 'voluntary' and 'forced' migrations and also offering a paradigm with which to analyse diverse forms of migration. Richmond argues that it is no longer tenable to treat refugee movements as completely independent of the global economy. He suggests that it is not necessary to invoke Marxist analyses to 'recognise that the crises which have occurred in the Middle East, Central America and Asia are unrelated to the ideological and military confrontation of the superpowers, the competing interests of multinational companies and the problems of development facing Third World countries' (Richmond, 1988: 12). Using Giddens' structuration theory he goes on to argue that while all human behaviour is constrained, the extent of constraint is variable. Rather than using the terms 'forced' or 'voluntary' it would be

> more appropriate to recognise a continuum at one end of which individuals and collectivities are proactive and at the other reactive. Under certain conditions, the decision to move may be made after due consideration of all relevant information, rationally calculated to maximise net advantage, including material and symbolic rewards. At the other extreme, the decision to move may be made in a state of panic facing a crisis situation which leaves few alternatives but escape from intolerable threats. In between these two extremes people crossing borders will usually be responding to social, political and economic forces over which they have little control but will exercise a limited degree of choice about where they are going and when they go.
>
> (Richmond, 1988: 20)

Richmond's 'continuum', which basically rests on the argument that 'decisions regarding migration are more appropriately designated proactive or reactive, according to the degree of autonomy exhibited by the actors involved' (Richmond, 1988: 20), is particularly useful when we look at some of the 'new' migrations at a global level. The break-up of the Soviet Union in 1991 led many to predict a huge out-migration from East to West. Basically this has not happened and we must therefore ask why does migration not occur when there are obvious socio-economic reasons for it? Condagnone (1997) argues that migration theory 'must draw from and contribute to the current debate on agency and structure more than it has to date' (Condagnone, 1997:56). He goes on to suggest that the traditional lack of freedom of movement in the Soviet Union may be an important consideration here. Thus while post-Soviet migration has not been characterised by a huge rush for the 'West', there has nevertheless been a significant movement of ethnic Russians back into Russia from former Soviet republics, particularly those located in Central Asia. One attempt to unravel the 'new' migrations within the former Soviet space points to the complexity of the migrational process and the difficulties of distinguishing between 'forced' migration and voluntary migration. There has been a tendency to explain the out-flow of ethnic Russians from former Soviet republics as 'forced' due to the enactment of language and citizenship laws which discriminate against the ethnic Russian minority and which favour the titular nationalities of the 'nationalising' states. The Russian state enshrined this notion by passing a law on 'forced migrants' in 1993; this relates to Russian citizens who are seeking a permanent return to their 'historical homeland' and who can show that they have suffered violence or the threat of violence (Pilkington, 1997:103). Pilkington's field research among 'returnees' indicates that only half of those interviewed had in fact registered with the Federal Migration Service and therefore had been required to claim direct persecution. Rather the single most important motivating factor was stated as 'the future of the children', indicating that their migratory decision was made in anticipation of impending political and economic discrimination in the former republics (Pilkington and Phizacklea, 1999). This is where Richmond's continuum is useful, it provides us with a device for analysing the migratory decision in relation to the degree of autonomy exhibited by the actors involved. In the case of some Russian returnees migration is seen to be in the long-term socio-economic interests of the family, they are leaving 'peaceful' states but these are no longer 'Soviet' states and the Russian minority fear for their future well-being. For others migration is a reactive strategy to direct persecution or violence, for instance the ethnic conflict in Baku in 1990, which displaced both Russians and Armenians who 'fled' into Russia. Wherever they fit on the continuum they have by 'packing their bags' become border crossers or 'transnationals', but how easily do they fit within the term as it has developed within the literature, a term which suggests that something 'new' has been emerging objectively and needs to be conceptualised differently, in other words a 'real' rupture?

Transnationals?

Some would argue that a significant theoretical rupture has occurred in moving from a focus on the migrant's position in the 'host' country, commonly envisaged as being caught 'between two cultures', to a position where 'migrants have become icons of hybridity' (Salih, 1999:1). This re-emphasis is most marked in the literature now referred to as 'transnationalism' and defined as 'the process by which immigrants forge and sustain multi-stranded social relations that link together their societies of origin and settlement' (Basch *et al.*, 1994: 6). Transnationalism, Portes argues, allows people to lead political, economic and social 'dual lives' through the creation of 'dense' cross-border networks (Portes, 1997: 812). Vertovec argues that while these long-distance networks preceded the nation-state, contemporary transnational networks mark a new departure because they 'function in real time while being spread around the world' (Vertovec, 1999: 447). Portes also emphasises the importance of the 'newly acquired command of communication technologies' by individuals within such networks and that 'Participants are often bilingual, move easily between different cultures, frequently maintain homes in two countries, and pursue economic, political and cultural interests that require their presence in both' (Portes, 1997: 814). In fact in a later article, Portes, Guarnizo and Landolt argue that what makes 'transnationalism' a completely new phenomenon are the 'high intensity of exchanges, the new modes of transacting, and the multiplication of activities that require cross-border travel and contacts on a sustained basis' (Portes *et al.*, 1999: 219).

In the introduction to a book titled *Between Two Cultures* the editor states that 'To date most anthropologists have not really come to grips with the problem of class in complex societies' (Watson, 1977: 14). The same could be said of much of the literature on transnational communities. Portes *et al.* admit that if technological innovations represent a necessary condition for the rise of grass-roots transnationalism, it follows that the greater access of an immigrant group to space- and time-compressing technology, the greater the frequency and scope of this sort of activity. Immigrant communities with greater average economic resources and human capital (education and social skills) should register higher levels of transnationalism because of their superior access to the infrastructure that makes these activities possible.

(Portes *et al.*, 1999: 222)

It is an admission that such individuals had already a 'class' advantage. Bhachu's study of South Asian migrants in Britain emphasises the heterogeneity of class and caste positionings of these migrants. In the case of the 'thrice' migrants, from India to East Africa, from East Africa to Britain and then in the 1980s and 1990s their further move to countries such as US, Canada and Australia, it means that they possess

powerful communication networks, which are facilitated by the ease of global communications. Their command of Western bureaucrat skills and the English language has given them considerable expertise at reproducing their cultural bases and community infrastructures in a range of countries. Such a scenario is in complete contrast to that of the less 'culturally and ethnically skilled' direct migrants, who are often characterised by home orientation and the 'myth of return'.

(Bhachu, 1995: 224)

The resort to transnationalism 'from below' as a method of countering and subverting the logic of transnational capital may not be a strategy open to all. We cannot compare the fortnightly phone call and the desperately small amounts of money remitted by poor Sri Lankan migrant domestic workers in the Gulf States to the transnational business deals of the cosmopolitan entrepreneurs that we visit later in this book without recourse to a class analysis. To state this as obvious is not to return to the structural 'strait-jacket' of the neo-Marxist political economy accounts, it is simply to say that while all of these transactions are transnational, the actors involved have very different points of departure or degrees of autonomy over the nature of those transnational transactions.

Roberts *et al.* are perceptive in arguing that theories of transnational migration emerged in large part as a critique of

> overly structural approaches, and attempted to introduce the actor back into theoretical migration discussions. Countering a tendency to see migration as created by the push and pull of economic factors with migrants conceived as mainly as passive subjects, coerced by states and marginalised by markets, work on transnational migration attempts to impute migrants with decision-making capabilities influencing their outcomes.
>
> (Roberts *et al.*, 1999: 253)

This criticism echoes the standpoint of virtually all currently working in the field of migration who are keen to restore an analytically coherent view (rather than prolong the phoney war) of the relationship between structure and agency. The processes described by Portes and others are important features of contemporary global migratory patterns and the economic, political and cultural ethnoscapes that they represent. The question remains as to whether social scientists' current preoccupation with this supposedly 'new' category of international migrants warrants another theoretical rupture of the kind we seem to go through every five to ten years.

The subjective mark of the transnational would be cultural hybridity or the way in which transnationals can challenge the notion of a fixed identity. But again there is nothing completely novel about this; cultural studies as a discipline has for a very long time analysed the dynamic, hybrid cultures particularly evident in cosmopolitan urban spaces (for instance, Hall, 1991). Returning to Bhachu again, she argues that younger Asian women in the UK

> emerge from the particular localities in which they have been raised, and from particular class cultures to which they have been socialised. ... Whole facets of the existence of Asian women are subject to and determined by common economic, class and regionally specific forces, which have as much impact on the lives of

white British women as they do on Asian women, regardless of their various ethnicities.

(Bhachu, 1995: 238)

We certainly use the term 'transnational' throughout this book, but we do so to refer to the many and varied transactions and processes that migrants maintain between 'home' (as in 'where I was born') and 'home' (where I am now). These transactions may not take the form of building businesses which link the two or 'political and cultural interests that require their presence in both' (Portes, 1997: 814). In fact they are much more modest forms of transnationality, such as buying a phone card for the weekly chat (you buy the phone card that you can afford that week); possibly explaining that you will not be sending so much money back this month because you lost your job and, with it, your accommodation. But they also comprise celebrating certain events of importance 'at home' and maintaining certain other 'cultural' symbols, such as dance, food and religion in the new 'home'.

Conclusion

In this chapter we have looked at some of the ways in which theorists over time have conceptualised migration. We have suggested that the consequence of the supposed theoretical ruptures in that conceptualisation has often led to the complete jettisoning of some theories for others, rather than the retention of what is useful in some approaches and how that can be developed within the context of changing realities and 'fashions' in theory. We have suggested for instance that the migratory decision can be analysed within the context of the degree of autonomy exercised by the individual actor. Thus at one extreme we could be looking at the situation of refugees forced from their homes by genocidal armies, earthquakes or flood waters. At the other extreme we are looking at well-qualified, affluent migrants whose stock of human and cultural capital insures their unfettered global mobility. The interplay between the agency of the individual actor and the structural context within which that actor manoeuvres is at the heart of most studies of migration and in the next two chapters we want to look at how actors with differential access to power and resources manoeuvre within those structures.

Chapter 6

The politics of belonging

Sex work, domestic work: transnational household strategies

Annie Phizacklea

In the last chapter we looked at how the 'phoney war' between structural- and agency-driven accounts has been worked through in explanations of migration. We have suggested that there is no single theory which can encompass all types of migration but there are certain broader-based paradigms which provide more satisfactory frameworks. One we have pointed to is Richmond's where he argues that the migratory decision-making process can be regarded as a continuum with proactive migrants at one extreme and reactive migrants at the other, reflecting the degree of autonomy exhibited by the actors involved (Richmond, 1988: 20). The other paradigm which we will explore in more detail here is that of migration systems theory. The latter suggests that an understanding of any migratory movement necessitates our incorporation of macro-structural factors with micro-level structures, such as the family, social networks, the huge number of intermediaries now involved in the 'business' of migration and the individual migrant's motivations and understandings. At the macro level we would want to look at the processes of globalisation, the free movement of capital, the revolution in communication technologies and the linkages between sending and receiving societies at a time of increasingly restrictionist attitudes towards the entry of labour, refugees and asylum seekers in states at the 'core'. These macro factors will influence and interact with intermediary institutions such as informal social networks and more institutionalised agents such as recruiters, brokers and 'fixers'. They in turn interact with households and the individuals which make up that household.

In the last chapter we deliberately avoided bringing in what we might consider to be an intermediate level of analysis through a consideration of the role played by institutions such as the household and the social networks based on family, friends and community ties. In this chapter we want to turn attention to these institutions as well as the proliferation of employment agencies, immigration advisers, traffickers, etc., all of whom facilitate migration, employment and settlement in the migration setting.

Writing in 1989 Monica Boyd argued that 'current migration patterns and new conceptualisations of migration underlie more recent interest in the role of family, friendship and community based networks' (Boyd, 1989: 641). At the same time she argued that there was a need for greater specification of the role of networks in migration research and for the inclusion of women in future research. This chapter constitutes one attempt to do that in providing both a critique of extant theory and developing new ways of looking at how networks, including the household and intermediaries, link migrants and non-migrants across time and space.

Over the last decade a good deal of play has been made of the so-called 'feminisation' of migration world-wide. In *One Way Ticket* (Phizacklea, 1983) we were keen to correct what we considered to be a misplaced emphasis on migration as a largely male phenomenon with women getting a rare look-in as wives or daughters of male migrants. Even in situations where emigration data indicated quite clearly that during the 1950s and 1960s women were independent labour migrants (for instance from the Caribbean to the UK and France) their presence was ignored (see Phizacklea, 1982, for an analysis of labour migration from Jamaica). Thus when Castles and Miller claim that the 'feminisation of migration' has become, and will continue to be, an important tendency of transnational migratory movements, one response is that it always has been an important tendency. Nevertheless the quantification of transnational movements in a gendered way has become increasingly imprecise since the introduction of strict immigration controls in the affluent countries of the world since the early 1970s.

Some migration specialists challenge what they refer to as the 'conventional wisdom' that female labour migration has outnumbered male since 1974 (Zlotnik, 1995: 229). The argument is that 'the fact remains that the majority of women who migrate internationally do not do so for work purposes. That is especially the case of women migrating legally from developing to developed countries' (Zlotnik, 1995: 230).

On the basis of official entry data Zlotnik is correct; apart from professionals with scarce skills, it has been very difficult for anyone to migrate legally for employment purposes from the developing to the developed world since 1974. But if we examine the gender composition of regularisation programmes (the decision by nation-states to regularise the immigration status of people who for one reason or another are 'undocumented') over the last ten years then we can conclude that indeed women do constitute a significant proportion of labour migrants in transnational movements. Elsewhere there are figures to indicate the substantial numbers of women who have been regularised under such programmes (Phizacklea, 1999; DeLaet, 1999). It is important to recognise that when people speak of such programmes as 'amnesties' it gives the impression of governments simply opening the door to hundreds of thousands of previously 'illegal' migrants. Nothing could be further from the truth. For instance, for an individual to be even considered for legal permanent residency status under the 1986 Immigration Reform and Control Act in the US, they had to prove continuous 'illegal' residence in the US prior to January 1982. In the Netherlands the same criteria have to be met over a two-year period, and as we shall see in the case study of the maids' industry at the end of this chapter, the hurdles which domestic workers are currently having to jump through in the UK in order to become regularised are many and difficult.

Thus for the affluent countries of the world we can make some rough and ready calculations about numbers and trends and add to this the evidence of a massive increase in the number of women migrating legally from and within Asia over the last ten years (Castles and Miller, 1998; Anderson, 1997; Skeldon, 1999; DeLaet, 1999). However imprecise the picture, we cannot conclude that women migrants 'simply follow men' around the contemporary world.

Households, gender and migration

During the 1980s analysis of migration began to shift attention to the role of intermediary institutions in the migratory process, particularly the role of households and social networks.

It is often assumed that because women are members of households then bottom-up accounts of migration that start with household decision-making must provide more adequate accounts. In the early 1980s certain economists moved beyond models of migration predicated on individual rational choice to one where the 'family' was recognised as the effective decision-making unit (Stark, 1984 is an example of this; also see his Morgenstein Memorial Lectures, 1999).

There are those who see these 'new economics of migration' accounts as overcoming the shortcomings of neo-classical models based on individual, rational decision-making (see Cohen's introduction, 1996: xv).

Certainly households are an important unit of analysis in mediating between individual migrants and the larger structural context, but we also need an analytical shift which recognises that households are deeply implicated in gendered ideologies and practices. That recognition is missing in accounts such as Stark's. For instance, it is quite common to find the following assumptions in accounts of migration which utilise the household strategy model: that households represent shared income, resources and goals; that migration is a reactive strategy to a lack of fit between household consumption and locally available resources and that household-wide decisions are made about migration (see, for instance, Wood, 1982; Selby and Murphy, 1982).

In their book *The Age of Migration* (1998), Castles and Miller cite Hugo's (1994) research on Asian migration which shows that migration decisions are usually made not by individuals but by families. They go on to argue that

> In situations of rapid change, a family may decide to send one or more members to work in another region or country, in order to maximise income and survival chances. In many cases, migration decisions are made by elder (especially the men) and younger people and women are expected to obey patriarchal authority. The family may decide to send young women to the city or overseas, because the labour of the young men is less dispensable on the farm. Young women are also often seen as more reliable in sending remittances. Such motivations correspond with increasing international demand for female labour as factory workers for

precision assembly or as domestic servants, contributing to a growing feminisation of migration.

(Castles and Miller, 1998: 25)

Later in this chapter we will use recent interview data with migrant domestic workers in London, UK, to indicate that the factors governing the migratory decision are many and complex. Many of the women we have interviewed only told their families of their intention to migrate after they had made their plans. Others left to escape unsatisfactory or violent marriages. Others only discussed the plan with the individual whom they trusted to care for their children while abroad. Others refer to unspoken familial expectations of financial responsibility for younger brothers and sisters. Money and self-respect seem to be at the centre of these accounts. Reference to this empirical work presumably falls foul of Portes' view that 'A cautionary note must be introduced here about analyses that concentrate exclusively on the individual motivations of household members and the conflict of interests between them. This has often become the centre of gender-focused research' and he goes on to warn against 'making respondents' definitions of the situation the ultimate test for theoretical propositions' (Portes, 1997: 816). Portes does not make reference to the reason why a growing number of scholars have been keen to give women a voice, a voice which was previously never heard and which is often at odds with the overriding assumption in much of the literature that women simply follow men in the migration process or do what family men tell them to do. As Mary Evans argues, 'feminism can claim to have developed one of the now great critical traditions within the Western academy, that of suggesting that the universalistic assumptions of knowledge in our society are false, and partial, because they are drawn from the experiences of only one sex' (Evans, 1997: 122).

Thus some of the more recent accounts acknowledge for instance that 'The household, as we conceive it, has its own political economy, in which access to power and other valued resources is distributed along gender and generational lines' (Grasmuck and Pessar, 1991: 202). Also the household cannot be analysed in isolation from extra-household relations, in particular the social networks and other migrant institutions which support transnational migration (Hondagneu-Sotelo, 1995; Boyd, 1989).

Empirical work which has explored decision-making within households regarding migration points to the hollowness of the assumption that households make collective decisions. In her research on Mexican migration, Hondagneu-Sotelo shows that men who migrated ahead of wives and children did so quite autonomously with little regard for the rest of the family's views on this decision. Rather than the women who were left behind viewing this decision as based on a recognition of family need, they were in fact fearful that they might be abandoned altogether. As male remittances rarely met household consumption expenditure in Mexico, many women effectively became sole heads of households. The result was an increased desire by women to move North in order that husbands resume at least partial social and economic responsibility for family welfare. Hondagneu-Sotelo concludes:

> Opening the household 'black box' exposes a highly charged political arena where husbands and wives and parents and children may simultaneously express and pursue divergent interests and competing agendas. How these agendas become enacted draws attention to the place of patriarchal authority in shaping migration … a household cannot think, decide or plan, but certain people in households do engage in these activities.
>
> (Hondagneu-Sotelo, 1995: 95)

To reiterate, households do constitute an important unit of analysis in accounts of migration but there are a number of qualifications to their use; first, the problem of definition: what is a household and who is a member? Given the very different cultural meanings attached to the concept 'household' and the heterogeneity of family forms, there are real problems of boundary marking on a transnational basis. Second, households as a unit of analysis cannot be examined in isolation from the broader structural and ideological context within which they are situated, they can only be viewed as an intermediate unit of analysis which plays a part in 'the bigger picture'.

Given these qualifications, how useful can a focus on the household be in a gendered analysis of migration? If we are alert to the fact that once we open the household 'black box' we may in fact find a 'can of worms', then as a unit of analysis in what is a very complex account of why and how migration happens, it is very useful. Hondagneu-Sotelo's detailed research on Mexican families indicates clearly that households are not the cosy rational decision-making units that some accounts would lead us to believe. It is possible that the number of households who sit down around the kitchen table and discuss in a rational way who it is that will make the most money if they migrate is very small indeed. Goss and Lindquist have pointed out that this conception of the household is

> unlikely to be applied uncritically to Western societies and is consistent with the ideological tendency in social sciences to romanticise peasant and community in the Third World. Somehow, members of Third World households, not burdened by the individualism of Western societies, resolve to cooperate willingly and completely, each according to their capacities, to collectively lift the burden of their poverty.
>
> (Goss and Lindquist, 1995: 328)

Later in this chapter we will see that money is central to women migrants' accounts of decision-making about migration, but so is self-respect.

The role of remittances sent home to households (and it is important to recognise that the nature of the household may change a good deal with migration, for instance your children may go and live with your mother, or your mother-in-law, etc.) world-wide should never be underestimated. The Central Bank in the Philippines officially recorded remittances worth US$4.94 billion for 1995 alone and this does not take account of the many unofficial ways that migrants send money home (Anderson, 1997: 25). The economic status of a household is important in other ways, for instance we know that it is not the poorest individuals who are in a position to migrate, they neither have the means (which could even be the bus fare to get into the nearest urban centre) nor the contacts to facilitate a move (Pessar, 1982; Phizacklea, 1999). Finally, if a migrant can establish a reasonably secure base in the migration setting the possibility of other household members joining them can be considered. It is important that we think about the household in these ways rather than the conventional, one-dimensional view of wives entering under regulations permitting family reunion and the subsequent reconstitution of households in the migration setting. The latter is important, but it is only one way in which we can consider households in the migration process. Finally, what is happening to households of citizens in the destination sites of migration is equally important. As we shall see, women's changing aspirations for education, career and marriage, in many cases their reluctance to accept the responsibility for child and elder care, all have implications for the way households are constituted and have knock-on effects for contemporary migration trends, whether it be an increased demand for migrant domestic workers or a 'mail-order' bride. In short, the 'household' is a crucial concept in any account of migration but in very diverse ways and it is only one piece in a very complex jigsaw.

Social networks and migrant institutions

Boyd argues that

> A starting point for research on social networks is that structural factors provide the context within which migration decisions are made by individuals or groups. However, at this microlevel analysis, the decision to migrate is influenced by the existence of and participation in social networks, which connect people across space.
>
> (Boyd, 1989: 645)

The main arguments are that social networks comprising households, friends and community ties are crucial for an understanding of settlement patterns, employment and links with the homeland. Once migration begins these networks come to function as causes of migration themselves because they lower the costs and risks of migration and increase the expected returns on migration (Massey *et al.*, 1993). Networks constitute an important resource for migrants who use them to gain employment, housing, etc., in the migration setting. Without the existence of these social networks migration involves high costs and risks. Much of what is being described here is the phenomenon of chain migration or the passing of information from migrant to home, particularly information on job vacancies which may encourage family members and friends to devise ways of migrating and finding jobs in the migration setting. Undoubtedly, social networks are of immense importance in precisely the way Massey *et al.* describe; unless you hear about employment opportunities and can slot yourself into a 'tried and tested' employment destination, migration is a very risky business.

Social networks are also central to Hondagneu-Sotelo's analysis of Mexican migration where she concludes that

> Traditionally, gender relations in the networks have facilitated men's and constrained women's migration, but this is changing. While patriarchal practices and rules in families and social networks have persisted, through migration women and men reinterpret normative standards and creatively manipulate the rules of gender.
>
> (Hondagneu-Sotelo, 1995: 96)

If we consider migration to Britain from what was called the 'New Commonwealth' in the 1950s, the pioneers of that migration came to fill jobs that had either been advertised in their home countries or had been brought to their attention by the activities of recruiters. As these pioneers settled into work they sent home information about job opportunities. Potential migrants had at least some knowledge of where to get a job and an address where a brother, sister, cousin, close friend was living. The importance of social networks in facilitating migration is therefore well recognised, but their ability to articulate between structure and agency is questioned in another innovative account which draws our attention to the increasingly formalised nature of migration.

Goss and Lindquist argue that there is a mid-level concept which 'articulates' between various levels of analysis; they call this the 'migrant institution' (Goss and Lindquist, 1995: 317). Using Giddens' structuration thesis and applying it to migration from the Philippines, they argue:

> the key component of recent large-scale international migration, largely neglected in the literature, is the complex of international and national institutions that transcend the boundaries of states and locales, linking employers in the developed or rapidly developing

economies with individuals in the furthest peripheries of the Third World.

(Goss and Lindquist, 1995: 335)

As we will see in the analysis of the sex and maids industries, migration has become institutionalised in South-East Asia and, to some extent, the Indian sub-continent, from the state down.

The ensemble of social networks and intermediaries referred to by Goss and Lindquist as 'migrant institutions' is 'a complex articulation of individuals, associations and organisations which extends the social action of and interaction between these agents and agencies across time and space' (1995: 319). Giddens does not view structure as necessarily external and constraining to individual and collective agency. Quite the reverse because Giddens views structures as both constraining *and* enabling; as individuals, he argues, we make, remake and transform structures in the course of our daily lives (Giddens, 1984: 25). He also argues that while both knowledge and power are unequally distributed, even the seemingly powerless have the capacity to mobilise resources and secure 'spaces' of control.

Thus Goss and Lindquist argue that 'Individuals act strategically within the institution to further their interests, but the capacity for such action is differentially distributed according to knowledge or rules and access to resources, which in turn may be partially determined by their position within other social institutions' (Goss and Lindquist, 1995: 345). Basically they are looking at a situation where the Filipino government since the Marcos days has encouraged migration but also seeks to control it in a number of ways: in negotiating bilateral agreements, particularly with the Gulf States, by controlling remittances and in theory protecting the rights of workers abroad. Originally it also intended to monopolise international labour migration by cutting out employment agencies but it failed, so it now endeavours to control their activities through licensing (Goss and Lindquist, 1995: 338–9). Officially overseas employers must recruit through licensed recruitment agencies and any subsequent contracts be approved by the Philippine Overseas Employment Agency (POEA). Thus POEA-recognised recruitment agencies not only get licences, they get preference for contracts received directly by the POEA. But beneath this 'layer' there are unofficial brokers and fixers. Unless you have the money to go and stay in Manila how will you know what the possibilities are for jobs abroad? Fieldwork conducted by Goss and Lindquist in provincial Malinaw indicates that 'although 18 per cent of returning migrants claim to have obtained overseas employment without employing brokers, none managed without at least informal assistance of this nature' (Goss and Lindquist, 1995: 340). Skeldon cites a study conducted in 1991 which reports that two-thirds of domestic workers in Hong Kong had been hired though a recruitment agency (Skeldon, 1999: 10).

Goss and Lindquist argue that the more institutionalised migration becomes the more fraudulent and corrupt the system becomes. But despite this individuals still seek employment abroad. The authors conclude that

> Of course this is an indication of relative deprivation in the country but it is also the result of the selective flow of information through the migrant institution. Institutional agents control knowledge about the risks and disappointments of international migration, but it is obviously in their interest to hide these and to promote the advantages of overseas labour.
>
> (1995: 344)

While the notion of migrant institution works well for the case of Filipino migration where the process of migration has been to a large extent 'institutionalised', we would want to look carefully at the applicability of the notion of migrant institution in other situations where migration is far less institutionalised as a process. Nevertheless the Goss and Lindquist analysis is most certainly an advance in providing an account which can deal with the myriad of agencies and organisations now operating in the 'business' of migration.

In exploring what they term 'institutional theory' Massey *et al.* turn their attention to another aspect of the institutionalisation of migration. They argue that because affluent countries have introduced stringent immigration controls this creates a lucrative economic niche for entrepreneurs and organisations who will facilitate clandestine transnational population movements. Their activities include smuggling across borders, fake papers, arranged marriages, etc. In turn, because these practices create a highly vulnerable underclass of migrants, humanitarian organisations are set up to provide a range of services such as legal advice, shelter, help with obtaining papers.

Massey *et al.* conclude that these processes lead to a number of hypotheses which are completely different to those which emanate from micro-level decision-making models. They argue:

> As organisations develop to support, sustain, and promote international movement, the international flow of migrants becomes more and more institutionalised and independent of the factors that originally caused it. ... Governments have difficulty controlling migration flows once they have begun because the process of institutionalisation is difficult to regulate.
>
> (Massey *et al.*, 1993: 451)

Armed with this battery of extant theory we now consider two globalised industries, each representing the commodification of highly personalised and emotional relationships: sex work and domestic work.

Sex work, domestic work

If one asks a recently arrived migrant woman today where the opportunities for work lie in Europe, she will tell you that apart from sex work or domestic work, the avenues for employment are closed to her. There is now a widespread recognition that the restrictive immigration policies practised by virtually all states which receive migrant labour do not stop migration, they simply increase the number of migrants who are clandestine. This increase in clandestine migrant labour is not simply a feature of the traditional destinations for migrant labour such as the US and Europe, but now characterises much of the migration within Asia, a region where migration has rapidly increased alongside lop-sided development and industrialisation, some states experiencing wage rises and labour scarcity, others the exact opposite (Anderson, 1997: 2; Skeldon, 1999). Some of this industrialisation has opened up opportunities for women in export-oriented industries, making clothes, electronics, toys, etc., but the work is low paid and precarious; finding work abroad can present a more lucrative option. And there is no shortage of recruiters, nine out of ten foreign placements for Asian workers are handled by recruiters in some form, with an increasingly high proportion of those recruited now being women. To reiterate, a high proportion of these women will find themselves working in either the sex industry or working as domestics in a private household.

Over the last twenty years we have seen a rapid increase in the sex-related entertainment industry which has become an integral part of the tourist industry on a global basis. For instance, in Thailand it is estimated that two million women and children work in the sex industry, some of whom are migrants from Burma and Cambodia, while an estimated 50,000 Thai women work illegally in the Japanese sex industry (Anderson, 1997:16; Skeldon, 1999). Another 80,000 Filipina women work in the Japanese sex industry; in both cases the migration of women to Japan grew out of Japanese sex tourism. Now rather than the 'tourists' going abroad, the sex workers go to Japan on 'guest' visas which last for only three months. 'Deployment' costs to agents who set up the work and visas in Japan can be anywhere between US$15,000 and 20,000, which the women will have to pay off and which certainly cannot be paid off during the time span of the visa. Even when women can avoid prostitution as legal 'guests', they may be forced into it as indebted overstayers (Anderson, 1997: 28). Many of the accounts of sex work are harrowing in the extreme, so why do women get involved? For many there is a high level of deception, recruiters may say that the work on offer is waitressing or domestic worker. But Kempadoo argues that this is not always the case. Based on fieldwork in the Caribbean she argues:

> Sex work is another resource that women rely on to support and shelter themselves and families ... to buy a plot of land ... or to more generally improve the quality of life for themselves and kin. The amount they can potentially earn in the sex trade on a temporary short-term basis can be an initial pull and can be a retaining force.
>
> (Kempadoo, 1998: 128)

But she goes on to argue that while all migrant workers are vulnerable to exploitation due to their unfamiliarity with the migration setting, their lack of citizenship rights, their dependency on agents and racism in the migration setting, all of this is worse in the sex trade because of the outlawed nature of prostitution and the moral condemnation of commercial sex (ibid.:130). Skeldon also cites evidence to suggest that most women who work in the sex industry do so willingly and that those who are trafficked into slave-like conditions constitute a minority (Skeldon, 1999: 24).

The other large growth industry world-wide for migrant women is domestic work. The demand for domestic services world-wide has increased dramatically over the last ten years (Gregson and Lowe, 1994). As the number of dual-earner couples has increased in the affluent countries so too has the demand for maids, very often a demand which requires the domestic to live with the family. Rather than couples questioning patriarchal household and work structures (such as the 'man-made' day) and reorganising domestic labour and child-care on a shared basis, the preferred option has increasingly become one of buying in replacement labour for these chores. Women from poor countries throughout the world are now allowing couples in affluent countries to pursue well-paid careers without sacrificing children and all the comforts that the 'housewife' would have provided.

The classic illustration of this development was in 1993 when President Clinton in his zeal to find women to fill top jobs in his administration nominated Zoe Baird for Attorney General. It transpired that the Bairds employed an undocumented migrant woman as a live-in domestic worker and her husband, also undocumented, as a chauffeur. Not only were the Bairds breaking the law in employing undocumented workers, they also admitted to non-payment of social security and other taxes in respect of the couple (Macklin, 1994: 14).

The Baird case is not exceptional and research in the US suggests that while in theory it is illegal for employers to hire undocumented workers, in practice the Immigration and Naturalisation Service refrains from investigating such employers. This situation may be attractive for undocumented workers because they are less likely to come to the notice of the authorities if they are hidden in the privacy of the home, but it increases their exploitability as workers if the threat of deportation hangs over their head (Macklin, 1994: 30).

Research carried out by Anderson in five European countries in 1996 indicates that the practice of employing undocumented migrant women to carry out a wide range of domestic tasks is also widespread in Europe (Anderson, 2000). Not only are we looking at a situation in Europe of improving educational and employment opportunities for female European Union citizens, we are also looking at a situation of an increasingly ageing population (Walker and Maltby, 1997). In southern Europe welfare services are poorly developed and whereas in the past women in extended families would have been obliged to care for the elderly, the breakdown of the extended family and the obligations that went with it are leaving a very large gap. Countries such as Italy and Spain recognise the demand for domestic services in either regularising large numbers of undocumented domestic workers at frequent intervals or actually setting aside a certain quota of work permits every year for this occupation (as is the case in Spain, though the quota is usually used to regularise domestics already working in Spain). There is widespread admission that migrant workers are carrying out work that EU nationals are no longer prepared to do (such as live-in domestic work), for instance the OECD migration country report for Greece in 1994 argues that one in twelve employed persons in Greece is a foreigner:

> Most foreigners who work in Greece do so illegally. Immigrants without work permits can find jobs despite high unemployment. Their wages perhaps three to six times more than they can earn at home, are half the market rate in Greece ... foreign labour is used by many households for the care of small children and older people ... the large size of the informal economy and established networks that assist newcomers with information and accommodation contribute to the continuing flows.
>
> (OECD, 1995: 93)

It is of course a state of affairs which recognises that there is a two-tier labour market, one for EU nationals and one for nationals of 'third' countries who provide cheap and flexible labour power. But examining the social relations which characterise the employment of migrant domestic workers suggests reasons other than purely financial considerations.

Domestic service represents the commodification of highly personalised and emotional relationships, yet the employment of 'foreigners' for this job seems to mean that they can be treated with little or no respect (see Anderson, 2000 for a catalogue of examples). Migrant domestic workers have exactly the same concerns as their employers – they want their children to have a good education, they want a fair wage for a (long) day's work, they want to be able to socialise with their friends, they want (unlike their employers) to be able to buy a new jacket at the market; it is not just about money, it is also about self-respect.

The irony is that many of these workers are better educated and qualified than their employers. In the previous chapter we made reference to the fact that it is rarely the poorest or least well educated that migrate from poor countries in search of work or better paid work. This is why many have argued that migration is a kind of development aid from the South to the North, except that now it is increasingly horizontal as well, as the economic and political geography of the world changes. For instance, what were labour surplus countries and large exporters of labour, e.g. Italy, Spain and the Republic of Ireland, are now labour deficit countries. In the same way the 'new' migrations from the old 'communist bloc' and within the Asian and Pacific region testify to the rapidly changing and diverse sources of migratory flows.

Skeldon's research in the Asian and Pacific region confirms the findings of on-going research by Anderson and Phizacklea in London, UK and other research in Europe (see chapter 5). Educational level amongst domestic workers does vary by nationality, with Filipina domestics being particularly well educated. In Hong Kong Skeldon reports that 30 per cent of Filipina domestics have degrees, a further 32 per cent have some form of tertiary education and another 33 per cent have attended secondary school (Skeldon, 1999: 11). It is only among Indian and Sri Lankan domestics in Hong Kong that Skeldon reports significant numbers having no schooling at all but they are more likely to be working for Indian and Sri Lankan families (Skeldon, 1999: 11).

From this Skeldon concludes that

> the trade in domestic servants cannot be seen as simply the exploitation of poor working class women by newly emerging middle-class women, as the latter are absorbed into the urban labour forces in the developing economies of Asia. The vast

majority of domestics come from relatively better-off groups in the countries of origin and cannot be associated with a 'working-class'.

(Skeldon, 1999: 11)

But there is another interpretation which our empirical research in London leads us to draw. The shared experience of being an undocumented migrant domestic worker does lead to a form of 'class' identity which transcends differences of educational level, nationality, religion and language. Filipinas may be viewed as the 'preferred' nationality for domestic work, (particularly as they speak English) but this has not prevented, in the UK at least, their identification with other undocumented domestic workers irrespective of their nationality or religion. As we shall see in what follows, this shared experience constituted the basis of a successful campaign to regularise their visa status, a campaign that overrode diversity and difference in the migrant domestic worker labour force. In this instance the class dimension that mattered was their status as workers who came into the UK to work for rich transnationals. The UK case may indeed prove to be unique but it may also act as a model for other undocumented workers worldwide. We now turn to the specificity of the UK case.

Anderson and Phizacklea[1] are undertaking research with migrant domestic workers in London who are undergoing a process of regularisation of their visa status. On 23 July 1998 the UK government announced that it intended to regularise the position of migrant domestic workers who entered under certain immigration conditions and who had become overstayers due to no fault of their own. Specifically those conditions related to a concession introduced by the Thatcher government in 1980 which allowed foreign employers to bring in their domestic workers with them, but which tied those workers irrevocably to those same employers, they had no immigration or employment status of their own. The system was widely abused with one agency alone handling over 4,000 reported cases of imprisonment, physical and sexual abuse as well as widespread underpayment and non-payment of workers by their employers. Workers' usual means of redress was simply to run away from the abusive employer which immediately alters the conditions under which they were admitted and many, through no fault of their own, became overstayers. In short they joined the ranks of undocumented workers in the UK.

In 1979 the Commission for Filipino Migrant Workers was set up to support Filipino migrants in the UK, many of whom were domestic workers (Anderson, 1993: 59). The Commission increasingly gave support to domestics of many different nationalities who had left or wanted to leave abusive employers. While the Commission could provide support it became increasingly clear that immigration law as it applies to domestic workers who enter the country with foreign employers had to be changed. The domestic workers forged alliances with many other diverse groups, including trade unions, lawyers and other immigrant groups, to form KALAYAAN. The latter campaigned vigorously for ten years for the law to be changed and their efforts were rewarded in the policy change of 1998 proving yet again that even the seemingly powerless have the capacity to mobilise resources and 'carve out spaces of control'.

In what follows we want to draw on the ongoing empirical research to illustrate some of the theoretical points we have touched on in this chapter. In particular we want to draw attention to the gendered nature of the migratory decision, the shifting meanings of 'home' and the day-to-day reality of the politics of belonging.

The politics of belonging

In-depth interviews with seventy of the women undergoing regularisation and group discussions reveal a complex picture of how the migratory decision was arrived at and the heterogeneity of motivational factors. All the women interviewed in depth were asked who was consulted about the migratory project and how it was organised and financed. The following quotes illustrate the diversity of responses:

> I went to work in Manila as a domestic worker for a rich family, I met my husband there. He earns very little as a labourer and I didn't want my children to be like me. My friend knew of an agency that could find work in the Gulf, so we went together to the agency. I borrowed the money to pay for the flight and had to

pay the agency 12,000 pesos, 18,000 in total. My husband didn't want me to go.

(Filipina, 18 months in London, 10 years in Dubai, 3 children in the Philippines)

I left school at 16 and went to live with my aunt who was working in the Bataan Free Trade Zone. I joined her working in a clothing factory, thousands of people worked there making clothes for US firms. It was very long hours, but it was sociable, there were other people from my village and the surrounding area. I worked there for three years, it wasn't bad, the pay wasn't brilliant, but that's what everyone got and it was better than nothing, there was no work at home. But it was very monotonous as I only sewed one piece of the garment. Then a friend suggested that I went to the agency with him in Manila to find work abroad. My mother didn't want me to go, my supervisor in the factory didn't want me to go, but I borrowed money from my grandmother to buy the plane ticket. I used to send all my money home when I worked in the factory. I knew nothing about Kuwait and I was apprehensive, but I still wanted to go. In Kuwait there were three other Filipinas in the house so that helped with adjustment a lot.

(Filipina, in London since 1989, now married with one son)

I left school at 15 and I worked as a domestic worker before I got married. My husband had no work, he beat me, he's no use, he drinks. A friend found a family who needed a domestic and I came with them to England. I did discuss it with my parents and sister, I just wanted to contribute financially and my employers paid for the ticket.

(Indian, 12 years in London, 2 children in India cared for by sister)

My husband was a truck driver and a womaniser, he contributed little to the family and I decided that I'd be better off on my own, if I went to work abroad I could support my children. My mother-in-law lived close by and cousins as well, my mother-in-law was prepared to take responsibility for the care of the children. I attended high school until I was 14 years of age.

Having made up my mind to leave I went to an employment agency which was used by many others to find work in the Gulf. I had to pay 500,000 Rupees to the agency to arrange the job and I sold my sewing machine to help finance my trip, I financed my trip by myself. My youngest child was only 6 months old when I left for Saudi Arabia. The agency insisted that my husband signed a document saying that he was prepared for me to go abroad but he was more than happy to do that because my leaving gave him even greater freedom. My main reason for leaving to work abroad was financial, I could provide my children with better opportunities but I also knew that I was better off alone, so the decision was for me as well as the children. My mother did not want me to go but my mother-in-law had agreed to take responsibility for the children.

I went to work for a Prince in Saudi Arabia and I looked after the children from birth. It hurt me so much that as they grew up they showed me no respect, they even spat at me.

(Indonesian, left 13 years ago, 24 months in London, 2 children in Indonesia)

I lived in a town with my parents and eight brothers and sisters. It was a very close community. I attended secondary school and then completed three years at secretarial college graduating with a certificate in typing and office practice. I then worked as a secretary in Nigeria.

The pastor of our Church said that he knew of a diplomatic family in London who were looking for a live in domestic worker and were prepared to pay the airfare. I had already decided that I wanted to migrate and this was the opportunity, I also needed the money. I discussed it with my parents but I had already decided that this was something I wanted for myself.

The whole thing was arranged by others, the pastor and the employers in London. I didn't know anyone in London.

(Nigerian, in London 18 months)

The family I was working for in Accra were going to the UK for business and brought me with them. They suggested it. I told my mother that I didn't want to go with them but she said go, there's nothing for you to do in Ghana. I really was reluctant because they were not paying me in Ghana but they reassured me that I would be paid in the UK and that they'd be staying here for 4 years. I didn't feel I had much choice and they paid for my passport and air ticket. After 15 months in London, they still hadn't paid me, no clothes, no day off, not allowed out, nothing, just physical abuse. So I ran away.

(Ghanaian, 7 years in London, 1 child in London)

Thus, relieving poverty at home, building a better future for their children and escaping from unsatisfactory marriages are just some of the motivational factors for migrating. The key role that employment agencies play is significant amongst the workers from Asia and underlines the extent to which migration has become a business.

Most of the domestic workers interviewed in London fitted the classic model of the 'target' worker when they left their home country. The idea is to make as much money as possible to send home and to return home eventually. But migratory projects are often not that simple, those workers who left failing marriages know that their future is uncertain and not surprisingly they talk only of being able to go and visit home for holidays once they obtain their papers. Others meet new partners, have children and their financial links with the 'family at home' begin to be eroded as the option of 'living in' and the accommodation costs that this option saves evaporate and the cost of rearing a family in the migration setting begins to kick in. In the following extracts we can see how these differing pathways are experienced:

My children are grown up now but I phone them twice a month, I always send messages with my remittances and my children send me tapes. My family at home know that I am undocumented and they realise that if I get a visa I will be able to visit them for a holiday. My future is in the UK now, I want to stay here and work and be able to go home for holidays. My husband is dead now [died at 39 under mysterious circumstances]. I feel very much a part of the lives of those at home because of my financial contribution. That in itself has made me feel much more positive about myself, I can make a difference to their lives, the children have had education, they have their own house etc.

I feel very much that I belong in the UK now, I have many friends here of many different nationalities and I think British people are OK.

(Indonesian, left unsatisfactory marriage)

I phone home once a week, I'm eager to tell them about my son's progress, I send photos but my father says he really wants to see him. Without papers I'm worried about my child, when I get my papers I can go forward for the future, I'm going to be free and my son as well. I want to visit home but I'd like to study nursing here. I can't send much money home now that I have my son and the flat (£563 a month rent). But I do send money for gifts to my parents.

(Filipina, left 15 years ago, in London for 5 years with a 3-year-old son)

I keep in touch through letters, phone calls, I send messages with my remittances and when friends visit I get news of home as well. The amount of contact I have with home has stayed about the same over eight years. My family know that I am undocumented and they know what that means. I still feel a part of the lives of my family at home because I am contributing on a financial basis. Life abroad has changed me in every way and I see myself more positively now than before. After eight years in the UK I feel that I belong more in the UK than in India. I have many friends and my experience of British life and people is OK. I work for four employers and work 90 hours a week. I earn approx. £370 a month, rent is £30 a week but gas, etc., are included in the rent. I spend £10 a week on food, £12 on transport and give around £7 a week to the Church. My only other expenditure is on clothes. Three months ago I sent £250 home which cost £12 and I try and send that much every quarter. The money is sent to my husband and daughter for rent, food and schooling. I have no savings nor money in hand.

(Indian, 1 child at home in India)

> There was simply not enough money to go around, my husband
> was unemployed and we had many debts, so I had to find money.
> … I went to an agency to find work in the Gulf, my husband takes
> no responsibility for my daughter. She was 9 when I left and my
> brother and sister took responsibility for her. I phone every two
> weeks, I've paid off the debts and I support my daughter. I send
> my sister £800 every three months and that pays for my daughter's
> education. I think my life will change for the better when I get my
> papers, I'll be able to visit home and see my daughter, perhaps be
> able to bring her back here. I want to stay in London and be a
> beautician for which I am trained.
>
> (Indian, 1 child at home in Goa, India, 4 years in London)

For all of these workers the politics of belonging is a hugely
complicated affair. As far as the British state is concerned they simply
'belonged' to their employer and once they had left that employment
they certainly did not belong in Britain, they were just another group
of 'overstayers'. But now the state has changed its mind, it has
acknowledged that they should not have been allowed entry as mere
'chattels'. In the meantime, those same workers have lived and worked
without state support, have in all cases forged networks of friends and
in many cases have forged new lives with new partners and children.
For those who left children behind and who now have children in
London, the meaning of home and the politics of belonging become an
emotional nightmare.

The following extract is from an interview with a woman who was
married and had a child before she left the Philippines:

> my mother was happy to look after my son. I came to the UK with
> my employers, after four years I had to leave because I was
> pregnant. I live with my partner and my son, I feel at home here
> but I also feel at home in the Philippines, I just don't know how
> I'll feel when I go back. We want to get married but we don't
> have divorce in the Philippines so I'm still married to a Filipino.
> When I get my papers I want to visit my family straightaway, I
> miss my son so much. But what do I do? I would really like to
> bring my son back, but he regards my mother as his mother now,
> how would he adjust?, I so want him to be with his little brother. I

send money home twice a year for my son's education, I phone every two weeks and write once a month. ... I feel much more confident now, I have lots of English friends we met through play-group and baby sitting circles.

This worker already had a degree before she left the Philippines. Even though she is highly qualified she has been confined to domestic work since leaving 'home' because that was all that was on offer on the global labour market. But her life in London is lived through a lens that encapsulates at least three different settings. One is 'home' in the Philippines and the family including her son. The second is 'home' in London, where her 'English' friends do not know (because she has chosen not to tell them) that she is undergoing a slow, expensive and stressful experience of becoming documented. The third is her aspirational world, that includes updating her original professional qualifications in order to leave the world of domestic service behind her.

Permitting regularisation is only the first step in what has become an intricate, expensive and lengthy process for thousands of workers in London. But each step is also a process of empowerment. When we asked one woman what was she most looking forward to when regularised she said, 'not feeling panic when I see a policeman'. Yet many women have already had to pluck up courage and report their passports as 'missing' (meaning their original employer refuses to give them back their passport) to the police before their embassy will even consider issuing them with a new passport, the second step towards regularisation. They must provide evidence of employment from employers who are often extremely reluctant to admit to the employment of a domestic worker. The obstacles are many, but tackling each hurdle is in itself part of an empowerment process for each individual.

No one interviewed so far had ever dreamt the day they left home that they would end up as an overstayer through no fault of their own. Few of them fit cosily into the classic household strategy of migration model which assumes that households make rational decisions about who should migrate in order to maximise household returns. Most informed other members of households of their plans only after detailed arrangements had been made (usually through a recruitment agency for work in the Gulf States if they come from Asia) because for a range of reasons they knew there was no alternative but to migrate. Bringing a better life to their families is pre-eminent, sending home money to their families is their priority, but their own aspirations for the future are not just a better paying, legal job but the prospect of moving out of domestic work altogether. For some women a permanent return home is unlikely, they have left a failing or failed marriage and all the shame that comes with that admission in their home country, yet their responsibility to their children's welfare remains their priority. None of these women are victims in the sense that they ever passively accepted their 'lot in life', they left their homes, their families and everything that was familiar to sell their labour on the global market place. But they did more than simply operate as agents in their own right, they also acted as collective agents, they all stood firm in the campaign for regularisation, not least because they knew collectively that they had done nothing wrong, all they had expected was a wage (that had been agreed upon) and just a little bit of respect.

Conclusion

In this chapter we have focused attention on the role of those institutions and practices which link migrants and non-migrants across space and time. We have looked critically at the way in which the household is reified in many accounts of migration and why a gendered 'unpacking' of the institution allows us to retain it as a central unit without its reification. We have also seen that while social networks may be critical for an understanding of some migrations, they play a less central role for women in certain parts of the world, for instance Asia, where migration has become institutionalised from the state down. While there is a history of migration within and from Asia there is now considerable evidence to show that, for women at least, intermediaries such as employment agencies and brokers may be of more critical significance in facilitating, even institutionalising, transnational migration.

Some attempt has been made here to indicate where the main weaknesses lie in extant theorising from a gendered perspective and the case study of domestic workers hopefully indicates how the importance of moving between different levels of analysis is important if a more adequate account of the factors stimulating and facilitating migration is to be given. Perhaps more importantly this case study indicates that despite the harrowing conditions experienced by many women in the sex and maids industries world-wide, their migration represents an attempt to bring a better life to themselves and their families in the face of prodigious external constraint. It is in fact in the migration setting that the importance of social networks becomes clear, in the case of the campaign to alter the 1980 concession and to regularise the immigration status of those who entered under it. Without the solidarity that was generated across ethnic, religious and class lines amongst domestic workers themselves there would have been little chance of success.

Notes

A shortened version of the arguments in this chapter can be found in Kofman, E., Phizacklea, A., Raghuram, P. and Sales, R. (2000) *Gender and International Migration in Europe*, London, Routledge and in Ghatak, S. and Showstack Sassoon, A. (eds) (2001) *Migration and Mobility in Europe*, Basingstoke, Macmillan.

1   This project is being undertaken within the 'Transnational Communities' initiative of the ESRC in the UK.

Chapter 7

Economic ethnoscapes
Men, women and business

Annie Phizacklea

Introduction

In this chapter we want to explore the often complex social and economic dimensions of what is usually referred to as ethnic entrepreneurship. In particular we will argue that male migrants establish themselves in high-risk business ventures not because they are culturally predisposed to do so but because there is often little choice. If such entrepreneurs 'prefer' or 'choose' to work and do business with others of the same ethnic group, to what extent does this reflect a survival strategy in a hostile environment? To what extent do ethnic ties and solidarity have to be preserved and exploited as a resource and what does this mean for gender relations? In what follows we will focus attention on the proliferation of business start-ups in ethnic minority communities in Western economies over the last twenty years (Phizacklea and Ram, 1996). We will argue that in the face of industrial restructuring in these economies and subsequently much higher levels of unemployment in areas of ethnic minority residential concentration, migrants turned settlers have been forced to find new ways of making a living. But we will also argue that 'being your own boss' has become a more established route for many who believe that some career opportunities are blocked because of the persistence of racialised discrimination in many parts of the labour market. Nevertheless we also want to argue that the entrepreneurial route is largely confined to men. We use as case studies two very different sectors, the first is clothing manufacture where fiercely competitive pressures are passed on to a predominantly female workforce who work long hours for low pay. The second, enterprises which offer goods and services, which often, because of their location, serve a co-ethnic market and where commonly women's contribution to the business goes unacknowledged and unrewarded.

Gender and enterprise

We have spent some time attempting to correct a stereotype of migrant women that portrays them as passive followers of men, burdened by tradition (and lots of children). The women that we have considered working as sex or domestic workers are overwhelmingly independent economic migrants, who have made the decision to set out and sell their services on a global labour market. Even married women with children will grasp the opportunity of improving their families' economic position through labour migration, leaving their children behind to be cared for by relatives. Nevertheless before the introduction of stringent immigration controls many women did have the opportunity to enter affluent countries both as independent migrants and as spouses or dependants of male workers. While in many cases there was a waiting time stipulated for labour market entry of migrant women who entered as spouses they found their way in increasing numbers into the manual sectors of women's work in the affluent countries' economies.

The production of clothing has acted as a particularly important economic niche for successive waves of immigrants in many cities throughout the affluent world. If we look at New York or Paris or London we can trace the proliferation, though certainly not the inception, of small workshop and home-based production of clothing to the migration and settlement of mainly Russian and Polish Jewish communities from the 1880s onwards. In the period between the two world wars, and particularly in the immediate post-war period, large new factories were built in 'green field' sites throughout the advanced industrial world. These factories produced a far more standardised type of garment than those produced in the small inner-city 'sweatshops'.

But by the early 1960s we began to see the impact of what is usually referred to as 'the new international division of labour' where manufacturing firms seized the opportunity of reducing labour costs by shifting their production to low-wage labour sites.

While there were other incentives, such as tax holidays and restrictions on labour organisation in those low-wage countries who were keen to attract foreign employers, wages were deemed to be the single most important factor in attracting labour-intensive manufacturers away from the higher wage unionised countries (Hancock, 1983). Much has been made of the advantages to countries which in the immediate post-war period operated a guestworker system, such as paying nothing for the rearing or education of the worker, preventing costly family reunion and the fact that unemployment could be exported. But if workplaces were unionised the ability to use migrant labour as a type of 'reserve army' was limited. Most unions were not prepared to see 'a dilution' of wages in those sectors of work that they represented and collective bargaining agreements and/or minimum wage legislation largely denied employers the opportunity of using migrant workers to undercut wages. Nor were migrant workers on the whole happy about being treated differently. In the UK the 1970s marked a period of migrant worker resistance to allegations of white worker and trade-union racism and exploitation. In addition the competition for migrant workers in the advanced industrial countries of Europe had led to many concessions being made on issues surrounding, for instance, family reunion. After the rise in oil prices in 1973, most European countries imposed a ban on new migrant labour entries and many labour-intensive industries began to relocate to low-wage countries. The attractions of 'off-shore' sites were compelling, particularly in industries such as clothing production where 80 per cent of costs are in assembly and where the risks of mechanisation were deemed to be too high in those sectors subject to rapid fashion changes and unpredictability in demand.

The relocation of manufacturing production in industries such as clothing has not stopped over the last thirty years, but there have been, and continue to be, large national differences, which to some extent can be explained by the coincidence of changing markets and immigration policies.

For instance, countries such as the US, France and Britain have to differing degrees regarded themselves as countries of immigration and have permitted family reunion. Germany by contrast has always steadfastly proclaimed itself not to be a country of immigration and only reluctantly allowed family reunion. It is no coincidence that the small inner-city clothing manufacturers that exist in cities such as New York, Paris or London are dominated by ethnic entrepreneurs and labour, but are rare in German cities.

In the US, France and Britain, big clothing firms off-loaded their high-risk, unpredictable sectors of demand and maintained flexibility by increased sub-contracting domestically to the many small, inner-city firms while sub-contracting much of the more standardised production to 'off-shore' sites. The guestworker system in Germany recruited workers for specific jobs for which they were issued specific types of work and residence permits, the latter generally stating that the holder was not permitted to set up independently and family migration discouraged. In Britain, migrants from the New Commonwealth had originally the right to enter freely as did their spouses and dependants who also had the right to enter the labour market. Manufacturing job losses hit immigrant workers hard in the US, France and UK in the 1970s but there was nothing to stop those same workers creating alternative economic niches for themselves and their families. Very little capital is needed to set oneself up as a clothing producer if there is access to skilled, cheap and flexible labour. A good example of how this transition takes place is Coventry in the West Midlands. In the late 1960s there was no clothing production in Coventry, a city famed for its highly paid car production sector. By 1994 clothing production had become the only manufacturing growth sector in Coventry with Asian entrepreneurs dominating ownership of the eighty factories located in the city. One study carried out in the mid 1980s reported that some manufacturers in London were quite happy for their assembly work to be transported up the M1 because it was cheaper than relying on London sub-contractors (Phizacklea, 1990). Most firms increased the flexibility in their labour force by employing homeworkers on a highly casualised basis, a practice which has continued into the 1990s (Phizacklea and Wolkowitz, 1995; Felstead and Jewson, 1999).

Research carried out on homeworking in Coventry in the early 1990s indicated how deeply etched the racialised division of labour is in the homeworking labour force. Virtually all the Asian women homeworkers interviewed in Coventry were working in the clothing industry, none were to be found in the better paid, less onerous clerical work that white women had access to. Their sometimes higher earnings were not a product of better pay but explained by their working longer hours. In addition the work was unpredictable, reflecting the nature of the rush orders and short-run production that characterises their employers' business.

The ethnic differences in the homeworking labour force reflect national differences between white and Asian women. The latter were more likely to work full time, on average 48 hours a week, compared to an average of 26 hours amongst the white manual workers. On average white households who had fewer children to support were better off if homeworking earnings were excluded. Perhaps what is very telling is the difference in the responses of the Asian and white homeworkers when asked to name the advantages of being able to work at home. Not only did white women list numerous advantages, half said they preferred to work at home. While all the Asian women interviewed were first generation they had not recently arrived, indicating the difficulties they face in breaking out of low-pay ghettos such as manufacturing homework (Phizacklea and Wolkowitz, 1995).

Women who work outside the home in clothing factories also face low pay and long hours. But there is mixed evidence of the working conditions and level of control exercised by management and their attitude to their workforces. Earlier research carried out by Hoel in the Coventry clothing industry paints a very depressing picture with one entrepreneur expressing the view that

> I see the majority of women working for me as benefiting from my job offer. They are illiterate and have no skills, hence no British factory will make use of them. Their £20 a week will help towards the family income and we are like a big family here.
>
> (Hoel, 1982: 86)

In contrast Ram describes a shopfloor culture where the women exercise a degree of control over the organisation of work and are able to negotiate working hours with management (Ram, 1994). Nevertheless there is little evidence in the US, Britain, France or the Netherlands (where similar ethnic economies in clothing had developed) that women were becoming the entrepreneurs, it was men who were bosses and women remained largely workers, at best supervisors in these small sub-contracting firms (Morokvasic, 1987; Phizacklea, 1987).

It is interesting that commentators in the field of 'ethnic business' implicitly accept this sexual division of labour as 'normal':

> The 'captive' labour supply provided by immigrant wives, whose way of life keeps them largely separate from the wider society, is vital to the success of the enterprise, as is the interest of the potential entrepreneurs in accepting low wages for their work in return for gaining the experience which will equip them to set up their own in due course.
>
> (Mars and Ward, 1984: 4)

The fact that the fringe benefit of entrepreneurship is reserved for men is not questioned.

The question then arises as to whether this kind of business will survive subsequent generations. What happens when your specifically immigrant labour force runs out? Are sectors such as clothing production with low entry barriers simply a stepping stone to new and bigger businesses? The answers to these questions also present us with a mixed picture. Writing in 1999, Surinder Kaur (whose job covers monitoring pay and conditions in the West Midlands (UK) clothing industry and providing advice to clothing workers) argues that despite the fact that many of the larger firms have moved into a situation where they now control all aspects of the manufacturing process and have become successful exporters:

> The persistence of a 'poor' image will do little to encourage young workers into the industry and hence for the survival of the industry real changes need to be adopted. The perpetuation of low pay and poor terms and conditions of employment which seem to go hand-in-hand, does little to encourage new recruits into the industry and build up the self-esteem of those already employed. Quite often we are told by workers that they would like to work in other industries but are prevented from doing so because of their race, gender and inability to attend training programmes as their incomes are vital to the home.
>
> (Kaur, 1999: 12)

In addition as all the affluent countries now operate a system of stringent immigration control there exists a steady flow of people who enter such countries usually quite legally (for instance as students or tourists) but who become overstayers and who will seek work which is unrecorded. No one knows just how many undocumented workers there are in the inner-city sweatshops but these are the most vulnerable members of the workforce. In her study of the Parisian garment industry, Morokvasic exposes the punishing conditions that the undocumented work under:

> Slavica [is] a skilled garment operator from Yugoslavia, joined her boyfriend in Paris and found work in an atelier as a machinist. She was expelled three times from the country until finally she married in order to get at least a resident's permit. Still without a work permit she found a Yugoslav entrepreneur who agreed to give her work to do at home. She was hardly paid. After a year she joined workers in her atelier, 'he made us sit at our machines sometimes 60 hours a week, we had to because he threatened to break our contracts and we knew he had in reserve other home-workers waiting to replace us'.
>
> (Morokvasic *et al.*, 1990: 174)

Embedded business

But what of the entrepreneurs themselves? Are some ethnic groups more culturally predisposed to business than others? Can economic relationships be based on and be an expression of ethnicity? To what extent do individuals prefer to enter and do business with others whom they know and trust through kinship or ethnic ties?

Nearly thirty years ago Edna Bonacich put forward an explanation of why some ethnic groups are more likely to be entrepreneurs than others. She argued that groups who see themselves as temporary migrants are more likely to occupy a 'middleman' position such as independent trading or commercial activities in any context. Such groups will promote hard work, risk-taking and indirectly they will encourage the retention of ethnic solidarity which aids business activities. In a later work with John Modell they argue that certain groups, Jews, Chinese and Indians, will occupy this role and use ethnicity as a resource regardless of context (Bonacich, 1973; Bonacich and Modell, 1980). Other explanations for the growth in entrepreneurship amongst ethnic minorities stress 'push' factors, such as racialised discrimination in obtaining mainstream jobs and unemployment. In the UK Modood *et al.* (1997) argue that when looking at the growth of self-employment amongst South Asians we are probably looking at a very heterogeneous picture. At one end of the spectrum there are Indian and African Asian entrepreneurs, a third of whom have degrees. Both Westwood (1988) and Tambs-Lyche (1980) argue that in the case of Gujarati men (many of whom will have come to the UK from East Africa) their masculinity is constructed in relation to enterprise, trade, profit and abilities in the world of business. Thus self-employment and the building of a successful business will bring status within the community and constitute a strong 'pull' factor. In other words we are looking at minorities who over time have accumulated business skills and who have added to these certain relevant qualifications, often through higher education. In contrast Modood argues that four out of ten Pakistani and Bangladeshi self-employed had no qualifications at all. For these groups the contraction in employment for those with few or no qualifications but with access to the resources of kin and community may mean they have been 'pushed' into self-employment.

In the UK all South Asian minorities are over-represented amongst the ranks of the self-employed when compared to whites. In fact a third of the men in these ethnic minorities are self-employed in some way. By comparison only one in eight of Caribbean men are self-employed and women generally, excepting the Chinese, have low levels of self-employment (Modood *et al.*, 1997: 122). Some of the discrepancies in this very mixed picture may be explained by a vicious circle of stereotyping along gender and ethnic lines. A business start-up project targeting the West Midlands clothing industry found reports of negative racial and gender stereotyping by advisers and financiers as to the competence of women and black people to manage a business successfully (Kaur and Hayden, 1993: 101). In a five-nation European study of entrepreneurship amongst migrant women, Morokvasic argues that despite the strength and determination of the women interviewed to succeed, the largest obstacle they faced was overcoming the stereotype of migrant women as 'problems' (Morokvasic, 1988: 99).

In the West Midlands project over 70 per cent of the Caribbean male and female clients were unemployed and over 50 per cent of the whites. In contrast, over 50 per cent of the Asian men who came for advice were already in employment. The authors argue that

> While not ignoring the discrimination all Asian people face within the labour market, these figures would seem to confirm a commonly held view that Asian men often view self-employment as a positive alternative to employment and are more likely to receive financial and family support to pursue this path.
>
> (Kaur and Hayden, 1993: 106)

The debate between 'push' and 'pull' factors in business start-ups was explored in a pilot project by Phizacklea and Ram in 1994 in the twin cities of Birmingham, UK and Lyon, France (Phizacklea and Ram, 1995, 1996). The ten businesses studied in Lyon were all owned by North African men and seven out of ten of the businesses in Birmingham were owned by men of Pakistani ancestry, the remaining three were Indian. All of the businesses were located in the service sector, thus in Lyon there was a bakery, a halal butcher, a patisserie, a bazaar selling fancy goods, a video rental shop, a market trader, a garage owner, a café and a security business. In Birmingham the firms represented were a grocer, a clothes shop, a sweet shop, a printers, a video rental shop, a carpet shop, a market trader, a garage owner, an estate and travel agency and a sports shop. All the proprietors were male, the garage owner in Lyon entered a 'family business' as did four of the men in Birmingham.

When the proprietors of the business were asked why they had entered business, the vast majority indicated that either unemployment or the inability to find employment commensurate with their qualifications had been the motivating factor. Half of the Birmingham proprietors had degrees and complained about the blocked opportunity structures that they had experienced in gaining mainstream employment:

> I remember a white colleague of mine had a lower degree than I had and he applied for a job and got in and I didn't get a job. Well I had to adjust, I had no option; you've got to work to be successful

... you can't just sit on your bum even if you are academically qualified. If you can't get the job that you want you have to look for another job.

(garage owner, Birmingham)

It was more likely in the British case (four) than in the French case (one) that the existence of a 'family business' provided a ready-made escape route from unemployment. This resulted in the British case of an economist making and selling sweets, a biochemist selling Axminster carpets and a software engineer selling holidays and houses. Joining the family business had not been their first choice. In Lyon, unemployment was the motivating factor for most of the men in Lyon: 'I started the business 3 years ago, because there was no work, no jobs for immigrants' (bazaar, Lyon).

Not one of the twenty gave entrepreneurial 'pull' factors as a reason for going into business nor did any demonstrate what could be described as a cultural predisposition towards business. Whatever the level of education it was a case of 'push' factors that provided the motivation to go into business.

All of the businesses were located in depressed inner-city areas and apart from the garage owners relied upon customers who themselves were experiencing unemployment or who had very little disposable income and who were predominantly ethnic minority. Nevertheless the firms neither had the finance to move to more up-market areas nor in both cities were they confident that they could capture sufficient customers from the ethnic majority to make a success of the business in a different location:

It's crystal clear why I don't have many European customers ... even if they find items in my shop at half price they wouldn't buy them, they'd pay twice the amount to buy them from their own and that has its base ... racism.

(bazaar, Lyon)

Some only come in if the French shop is closed, between 1 and 2. 30, Sundays and Bank holidays. But when the French guy in the corner shop opens up at 2.30 they go there.

(grocer, Lyon)

In the conclusion to his 1991 study of ethnic minority businesses in Lyon, Abdelkader Belbahri argues:

> The Maghrebians experience the most tension between an indi-vidualistic approach to entrepreneurship and the need for a net-work of solidarity. In other words their position in society leads them to want to shake off their 'ethnic' group, for their enterprise to be 'ordinary' (not ethnic) but the constraints of the market and competition push them back towards the community of their origin. We have had the notable example of the Algerian printer who above all else wanted to be 'professional like the others', wanting to have nothing more to do with the 'Arabs'. But as he had no French customers he had to fall back on Maghrebian tradespeople and entrepreneurs for custom.
>
> (Belbahri, 1991: 58)

To reiterate, the notion of social embeddedness when applied to business relates to a preference by individuals to enter business or do business with others they know and trust either through family or other kin, social networks and membership of a close-knit community. The literature on ethnic minority businesses has embraced this notion, stressing in particular how ethnicity as a sense of group belonging and identification can act as a powerful resource in providing capital, labour and custom (Waldinger *et al.*, 1991). Ethnicity then becomes embedded in economic relations. But as we have seen, ethnicity also becomes embedded in racialised relations. The reluctance of the ethnic majority to trade with such businesses or the reluctance of banks to lend them money because they do not think they will manage the business in a competent way are just two examples of the way in which that works. In Lyon the interview questions which enquired about the involvement of banks as sources of start-up capital were met by gales of laughter. In Lyon the proprietors had relied either on family and other kin or a business start-up agency specifically targeting the unemployed to get access to the capital they needed. The baker in Lyon felt that the behaviour of banks was discriminatory:

> I went to see almost every bank, they said I needed more security. Well my parents have got a villa, I wanted to use that but they

weren't keen. I went to the Caisse d'Epargne, my parents, my brothers, we've all been with them for ages but they said no. I think if you're not French it's very, very hard. We face a lot of difficulties. I know a lot of French people who've got nothing, no support, nothing, who've had less trouble than I have had. Well I'm not thick you know, I see it straight away. Why should they be able to get credit so easily and not me?

Given the limited involvement of banks in providing the initial loans to ethnic minority businesses in France, there is a growing trend to turn to the more recently created business start-up agencies who are actively working towards helping the 'disadvantaged' (Simon, 1993). Such agencies cannot advertise themselves openly as providing assistance to ethnic minorities. If they want to do so they have to locate to areas of high residential concentration of ethnic minorities. The latter are not officially acknowledged in France because of the principle of universalism, you are either a foreigner or a French citizen. It takes no account of the fact that some French citizens are racialised and therefore the recipients of racialised discrimination. The researchers did interview bankers in both cities; in France these interviews were not reassuring. In Birmingham far more so, which is reflected in the greater willingness of the high street banks in the UK to lend to Asian businesses.

Finally we want to return to the hidden gender relations embedded in these 'family businesses'. Only one business in Birmingham employed non-family labour, the sweet shop, and one in Lyon, the garage.

They were very much family businesses but a recurrent feature of the interviews conducted with proprietors in both countries was the unacknowledged or grudging admission of the role of women in the business; the following was fairly typical:

> 'I take care of everything, well there's one thing I hardly touch at all and that's the paperwork, my fiancée does that, actually she's indispensable for the management side.'
> 'Do you pay her?'
> 'No!, she does it for me because I haven't got the time. In fact she takes care of *everything*.'
> (North African garage owner in Lyon: Phizacklea and Ram, 1996: 334)

Given the opportunity, the women in these 'family' businesses were very clear about their contribution to the viability of the business even though it was not registered in their name. Women's understandings of the 'firm as the family' should not be ignored, nor the ways in which predominantly female labour forces in ethnically homogenous businesses may negotiate their own 'women's' space, take pride in their work and recognise their crucial contribution to household income.

In Birmingham the printing business was registered as such and the proprietor conducted the initial interview as though there was no other business activity involved. However, it was clear that the printing business was only part of the outfit with a busy stationery section sharing the premises. After some careful questioning it transpired that the printing business contributed a mere 20 per cent of profits, the stationery business, run by the wife and daughter, providing the 'powerhouse' of the business.

Women are rarely registered as the sole or joint partners in these small businesses, but this is not to say that they do not recognise their contribution to the business and sometimes resent the way in which it is taken for granted. The only daughter in the grocer's in Birmingham (which also had a huge fruit and vegetable section on the street) kept a diary of her working week for purposes of the research. Her week was a mix of college studies and work in the 'family' business. At the end of one Saturday she recorded this in her diary:

> I personally feel that one of the major problems in the business is the issue of sexism. The reason for this is that my mother and myself are always the ones who are constantly working in the business on the serving side. I have to juggle working in the firm, doing the household chores and study at the same time. This is particularly evident on a Saturday when my mother and myself work from 8 in the morning until 7 at night, we then have to cook for the family, while the men do nothing at all all day!

All of the proprietors made it clear that there were considerations such as 'trust' and 'respect' in the deployment of family members that were as important as the fact that it was usually unpaid. And as we have seen most would grudgingly admit that wives' and daughters' labour often underpinned the competitiveness of the enterprise. But it is also clear that simply being taken for granted can cause resentment amongst family members whose contribution is rarely acknowledged to the outsider. This interpretation of 'reality' is contested by researchers working in other countries. David Ip and Constance Lever-Tracey in Australia argue that the role of women in family businesses has been misconstrued, that the view that men are entrepreneurs and that the women in such businesses are unacknowledged labour or 'partners' 'have not been supported by substantial evidence to date' (Ip and Lever-Tracey, 1999: 60). The only response to this view is 'yes', there is little research that even bothers to address these questions, and 'no', the research that has bothered to ask those questions over time, in the European context at least, does not paint a very optimistic picture of gender equality in so-called 'family' businesses.

Transnationals?

We have been at pains to argue against a stereotype of Britain's South Asians as a thrusting entrepreneurial minority who are somehow endowed with an entrepreneurial spirit that other minorities lack. We have also been at pains to suggest that many of the enterprises operate on incredibly low profit margins. Nevertheless it would be equally wrong to paint a picture of an undifferentiated lumpenbourgeosie struggling along near the poverty line. There is at least some evidence of a growing transnational group of wealthy global entrepreneurs. For instance, the *Sunday Times* 'Rich List 1999' lists many 'transnationals' such as the Hinduja Brothers based in London whose current wealth puts them at number 8 in the 'Rich List' in the UK. They are 'transnationals' in the sense that their father moved from Bombay (Mumbai) as a trader to Iran but insulated himself and themselves from the overthrow of the Shah through 'diversity'. They kept their 'foothold' in India: 'their strong position in India is a positive advantage as the economy opened up to foreign capital. In at least three of their sectors large multinational suitors are offering huge sums for equity stakes in Hinduja operations' and so it goes on: 'The Hindujas are also expanding their software operation from Bangalore, India's Silicon Valley, to Britain and the United States ... that is how to build an empire. ... The Hindujas would race much faster up this list if they were not diverting such large amounts of their wealth to charity –

between £45–60 million a year' (*Sunday Times*, 11 April 1999). The 2000 'Rich List' even provides a special column for 'The richest Asians' (*Sunday Times*, 19 March 2000: 20).

Conclusion

Much is made of the hard work and resilience of ethnic entrepreneurs in Western economies. As we have seen in many cases they have built thriving manufacturing industries, such as clothing, in what were fast becoming manufacturing deserts. Arriving with little money in their pockets they either set about building businesses where entry barriers were low or in the face of unemployment or blocked employment opportunities they 'fell back' on the business route as a survival strategy. There is some limited evidence to suggest that for some ethnic groups that 'being your own boss' is an important facet of the social construction of masculinity, for instance Gujarati men in the UK. Nevertheless we would need to look carefully at the backgrounds of these entrepreneurs and the position they occupied in the social structure of the pre-migration setting. In the case of Gujarati men in the UK a substantial number would have arrived from East Africa with commercial and trading experience and their presence would have an important influence on the ways in which other Gujarati men were integrated into the British economy. The same could be said for those Vietnamese who arrived in France in the 1960s and who were welcomed precisely because they had come from entrepreneurial backgrounds. But in the main there is little evidence to support the thesis that certain ethnic groups are more likely to have a cultural predisposition towards enterprise than others. In the clothing industry we have seen how successive waves of immigrants have carved out an economic niche which provides employment for family and co-ethnics. Competition is cut-throat at the bottom end of a sub-contracting chain, where profitability can only be maintained by securing a predominantly female labour force who claim they have little choice but to work in these enterprises or in their own homes given the gendered and racialised nature of mainstream labour markets. In the service sector ethnic minority businesses often occupy marginal economic niches abandoned by big firms and shops and survive through working long unsocial hours for meagre rewards. The description of 'family business' is an accurate one for most such enterprises but it needs to be recognised that it is often unpaid family women's labour that contributes to the viability of the business. Women are very clear about their contribution, but their husbands and fathers often made a grudging admission of it.

Finally, there is also evidence that entrepreneurship can result in the 'rags to Mercedes' phenomenon (though many in the 'Rich List' were part of a cosmopolitan business elite already). But we should not let the media preoccupation with the 'super rich' cloud our understandings of the social and ethnic heterogeneity of what the term the 'Asian community' represents, nor the very different class backgrounds that this term encompasses. The media is not interested of course in the 'hand-to-mouth' businesses that we have focused on in this chapter.

Afterword

We have attempted in this book to explore the contradictions and limitations of an understanding of the world as globalised and postnational. What we find is that far from a world without nations, the nation is fast being reinvented through many sites from governmental organisations to the popular press. For example, faced with the growing numbers of refugees and asylum seekers arriving in Britain, newspapers like the *Sun* have gone into battle against the newcomers. On 19 March 2000: 'The *Sun* announced "victory" for the 52,876 readers who supported its "Britain Has Had Enough" campaign to rid the country of gypsy beggars' (quoted by Fonseca in the *Guardian*, 24 March 2000: 2). The *Sun* appeals to a constituency which may or may not exist but it is created through this medium as a representation of the British public. This is of course an old story, for many centuries Europe's 'gypsies' have been vilified, demonised and ultimately subjected to genocide in the fascist period. The point of the story is that any account of globalisation and transnationalism which does not include an historical moment is deeply flawed and only fuels the residual racist discourses still so much alive in the world today.

These racist discourses insist that there is no space for a sense of belonging amongst asylum seekers and refugees. Instead, they must be on the move, shunted from border to border in search of a home and a safe place. These are the poor and the dispossessed of transnationalism. But they are not the totality. As the chapters here suggest there is another world, another circle which is building global networks and wealth through trade and business. Where these two come together is evident in the chapters on migrant domestic workers who provide services within the homes of the wealthy and who move around the globe with these families. Where, then, is home for these workers?

One area that we have only begun to explore here and is to be the subject of future work is the numerous ways in which globalisation has produced a counter 'anti-globalism'. This is, in fact, a growing phenomenon expressed in the attempts by different groups throughout the world to claim an essential and authentic political space very often through the global network of the World Wide Web. Prominent amongst these groups are the racists with their hate sites like White Pride World Wide or fundamentalist Christian groups. However, they do not have the only voice and the campaigns to end Third World Debt, to protect the rainforest and like minded groups are also using global forms of communication in order to critique global capital and its governance in the form of the World Bank and the IMF.

Bibliography

Adam, B. (1995) *Timewatch*, Cambridge, Polity Press.

Althubaity, A. and Jonas, A. E. G. (1998) 'Suburban Entrepreneurialism: Redevelopment Regimes and Coordinating Metropolitan Development in Southern California', in Hall, T. and Hubbard, P. (eds) *The Entrepreneurial City: Geographies of Politics, Regime and Representation*, London, Wiley.

Andall, J. (1996) 'Catholic and State Constructions of Domestic Workers', paper presented to the ERCOMER conference, Utrecht, Netherlands, April 1996. (Revised version published in Koser, K. and Lutz, H. (eds) (1997) *The New Migration in Europe: Social Constructions and Social Realities*, Basingstoke, Macmillan.

Anderson, Bridget (1993) *Britain's Secret Slaves*, London, Anti-Slavery International.

Anderson, B. (1991) *Imagined Communities: Reflections on the Origins and Spread of Nationalism*, London, Verso.

—— (1997) *Labour Exchange: Patterns of Migration in Asia*, London, Catholic Institute of International Relations.

—— (2000) *Doing the Dirty Work: The Global Politics of Domestic Labour*, London, Zed Press.

Appadurai, A. (1995) 'The Production of Locality', in Fardon, R. (ed.) *Counterworks: Managing the Diversity of Knowledge*, London, Routledge, pp. 204–25.

—— (1996) *Modernity at Large: Cultural Dimensions of Globalization*, Minneapolis/London, University of Minnesota Press.

Archetti, E. P. (1994) 'Masculinity and Football: The Formation of National Identity in Argentina', in Guilianiotti, R. and Williams, J. (eds) *Game Without Frontiers: Football, Identity and Modernity*, Aldershot, Arena.

Banks, M. (1992) *Organizing Jainism in India and England*, Oxford, Clarendon Press.

Basch, L., Glick Schiller, N. and Szanton Blanc, C. (1994) *Nations Unbound*, Langhorne, PA, Gordon and Breach.

Bauman, Z. (1998) *Globalisation: The Human Consequences*, Cambridge, Polity Press.

Beck, U. (1992) *Risk Society: Towards a New Modernity*, London, Sage.

Belbahri, A. (1991) *Les entrepreneurs étrangers dans l'agglomération Lyonnaise, Étude realisée pour le compte de Réseaux pour le Développement de l'Entreprise*, Lyon.

BELC (1976) 'Les Femmes immigrées et la formation', *Migrants-Formation*, No. 14–15, March.

Besserer, F. (1998) 'A Space of View: Transnational Spaces and Perspectives', paper presented to the ICCCR Conference on Transnationalism, Manchester, UK.

Bhabha, J., and Shutter, S. (1994) *Women's Movement: Women under Immigration, Nationality and Refugee Law*, London, Trentham Books.

Bhachu, P. (1995) 'New Cultural Forms and Transnational South Asian Women: Culture, Class, and Consumption among British Asian Women in the Diaspora', in van der Veer, P. (ed.) *Nation and Migration: The Politics of Space in the South Asian Diaspora*, Philadelphia, University of Pennsylvania Press, pp. 222–244.

Birnbaum, B. *et al.* (1981) *The Clothing Industry in Tower Hamlets*, Tower Hamlets Council.

Bloch, M. and Parry, J. (1989) *Money and the Morality of Exchange*, Cambridge, Cambridge University Press.

Bonacich, E. (1973) 'A Theory of Middleman Minorities', *American Sociological Review*, 38: 538–94.

Bonacich, E. and Modell, J. (1980) *The Economic Basis of Ethnic Solidarity: Small Business in the Japanese American Community*, Los Angeles and Berkeley, University of California Press.

Bonoli, R. (ed.) (1991) *L' Emigrazione al femminile: Atti del convegno*, Bologna, Regione Emilia-Roagna: Consulta Regionale per l'Emigrazione e l'Immigrazione.

Borjas, G. (1990) *Friends or Strangers: The Impact of Immigrants on the US Economy*, New York, Basic Books.

Boyd, M. (1989) 'Family and Personal Networks in International Migration: Recent Developments and New Agendas', *International Migration Review*, 23 (3): 638–70.

Breman, J. (1996) *Footloose Labour: Working in India's Informal Economy*, Cambridge, Cambridge University Press.

Brown, C. (1984) *Black and White Britain: The Third PSI Survey*, London, Heinemann.

Bundesanstalt für Arbeit (1980) Special issue: *Socialversicherungspflichtig beschäftigte Arbeitnehmer*, June 1979, Nuremberg, Germany.

Buroway, M. (1980) 'Migrant Labour in South Africa and the United States', in Nicholls, T. (ed.) *Capital and Labour*, London, Athlone Press.

Campani, G. (1993) 'Labour Markets and Family Networks: Filipino Women in Italy', in Morokvasic, M. and Rudolf, H. (eds) *Bridging States and Markets*, Berlin, Sigma.

Canclini Garcia, N. (1993) *Transforming Modernity: Popular Culture in Mexico*, Austin, University of Texas Press.

—— (1995) *Hybrid Cultures: Strategies of Entering and Leaving Modernity*, Minneapolis, University of Minnesota Press.

Carrier, J. (1995) *Gifts and Commodities: Exchange and Western Capitalism since 1700*, London, Routledge.

Carrithers, M. and Humphrey, C. (eds) (1991) *The Assembly of Listeners: Jains in Society*, Cambridge, Cambridge University Press.

Castells, M. (1975) 'Immigrant Workers and Class Struggles in Advanced Capitalism: The Western European Experience', *Politics and Society*, 5 (1): 33–66.

—— (1997) *The Power of Identity*, Oxford, Blackwell.

Castles, S. and Kosack, G. (1973) *Immigrant Workers and Class Structure in Western Europe*, London, Institute of Race Relations.

Castles, S. and Miller, M. (1998) *The Age of Migration*, London, Macmillan.

Castro, M. (1997) 'The Politics of Language in Miami', in Romero, M., Hondagneu-Sotelo, P. and Ortiz, V. (eds) *Challenging Fronteras. Structuring Latina and Latino Lives in the US*, London, Routledge.

Chant, S. and McIlwaine, C. (1995) *Women of a Lesser Cost*, London, Pluto.

Clark, A. K. (1994) 'Indians, the State and Law: Public Works and the Struggle to Control Labour in Liberal Ecuador', *Journal of Historical Sociology*, 7 (1): 49–72.

Cohen, P. (1988) 'The Perversions of Inheritance: Studies in the Making of Multi-racist Britain', in Cohen, P. and Bains, H. (eds) *Multi-Racist Britain*, London, Macmillan.

Cohen, R. (ed.) (1996) *Theories of Migration*, Cheltenham, Edward Elgar.

Condagnone, C. (1997) 'The New Migration in Russia in the 1990s', in Koser, K. and Lutz, H. (eds) *The New Migration in Europe: Social Constructions and Social Realities*, Basingstoke, Macmillan, pp. 21–39.

Crain, M. (1996) 'Negotiating Identities in Quito's Cultural Borderlands: Native Women's Performances for the Ecuadorean Tourist Market', in Howes, D. (ed.) *Cross-Cultural Consumption: Global Markets, Local Realities*, London, Routledge.

Da Matta, R. (1985) *Exploracoes: Ensaios de Sociologia Interpretativa*, Rio de Janeiro, Zahar.

Darder, A. (1998) 'The Politics of Biculturalism: Culture and Difference in the Formation of Warriors for Gringostroika and the New Mestizas', in Darder, A. and Torres, R. D. (eds) *The Latino Studies Reader: Culture, Economy and Society 1*, Oxford, Blackwell.

De Certeau, M. (1984) *The Practice of Everyday Life* (translated by S. F. Rendall), Berkeley, University of California Press.

Delacourt, J. (1975) *The Housing of Migrant Workers: A Case of Social Improvidence?*, European Commission, Brussels.

DeLaet, D. (1999) 'Introduction: The Invisibility of Women in Scholarship on International Migration', in Kelson, G. and DeLaet, D. *Gender and Immigration*, Basingstoke, Macmillan, pp. 1–20.

Department of Employment (1976) *The Role of Immigrants in the Labour Market*, Unit for Manpower Services, Department of Employment, London.

Diáz, J. (1996) *Drown*, London, Faber and Faber.

Dilley, R. (1992) *Contesting Markets: Analyses of Ideology, Discourse and Practice*, Edinburgh, Edinburgh University Press.

Do Nascimento, A. (1989) *Brazil: Mixture or Massacre: Essays in the Genocide of Black People*, Dover, MA, Majority Press.

Doezema, J. (1998) 'Forced to Choose: Beyond the Voluntary v. Forced Prostitution Dichotomy', in Kempadoo, K. and Doezema, J. (eds) *Global Sex Workers*, London, Routledge, pp. 29–34.

Donald, J. (1992) 'Metropolis: The City as Text', in Bocock, R. and Thompson, K. (eds) *Social and Cultural Forms of Modernity*, Cambridge, Polity Press.

Ecuador (1990) *Censos Nacionales 25 de Noviembre 1990*, Quito, Republic of Ecuador.

European Commission (1996) *Equal Opportunities for Women and Men in the European Union*, European Commission, Employment and Social Affairs, Brussels.

Eurostat (1997) *Statistics in Focus: Population and Social Conditions*, EC, Brussels.

Evans, M. (1997) *Introducing Contemporary Feminist Theory*, Cambridge, Polity Press.

Fawcett, J. T. and Arnold, F. (1987) 'Explaining Diversity: Asian and Pacific Immigration Systems', in Arnold, F. and Carino, B. V. (eds) *Pacific Bridges: The New Immigration from Asia and the Pacific Islands*, New York, Centre for Migration Studies.

Featherstone, M., Lash, S. and Robertson, R. (eds) (1995) *Global Modernities*, London, Sage.

Felstead, A. and Jewson, N. (1999) *At Home: In Work*, London, Routledge.

Fernandez-Kelly, P. and Garcia, M. A. (1997) 'The Politics of Work and Family Among Hispanic Garment Workers in California and Florida', in Romero, M. *et al. Challenging Fronteras. Structuring Latina and Latino Lives in the US*, London, Routledge.

Flores, J. (1997) 'Qué Assimilated, Brother, Yo Soy Asimilao', in Romero, M., Hondagneu-Sotelo, P. and Ortiz, V. (eds) *Challenging Fronteras. Structuring Latina and Latino Lives in the US*, London, Routledge.

Foner, N. (1977) 'The Jamaicans: Cultural and Social Change among Migrants in Britain', in Watson, J. L. (ed.) *Between Two Cultures*, Oxford, Blackwell.

Friedland, R. and Robertson, A. (eds) (1990) *Beyond the Marketplace: Rethinking Economy and Society*, New York, Aldine de Gruyter.

Gaffikin, F. and Nickson, A. (n.d.) *Jobs Crisis and the Multi-nationals: The Case of the West Midlands*, Birmingham, Trade Union Resource Centre.

Gelbard, A. H. and Carter, M. (1997) 'Mexican Immigration and the US Population', in Bean, F., De La Garza, R. and Weintraub, S. (eds) *At the Crossroads: Mexican Migration and US Policy*, Lanham, MD, Rowman and Littlefield, pp. 117–44.

Ghatak, S. and Showstack Sassoon, A. (eds) (2001) *Migration and Mobility in Europe*, Basingstoke, Macmillan.

Giddens, A. (1984) *The Constitution of Society*, Cambridge, Polity Press.

—— (1991) *Modernity and Self-Identity: Self and Society in the Late Modern Age*, Cambridge, Polity Press.

Goss, J. and Lindquist, B. (1995) 'Conceptualising International Labor Migration: A Structuration Perspective', *International Migration Review*, 29 (2): 317–51.

Granovetter, M. (1985) 'Economic Action and Social Structure: The Problem of Embeddedness', *American Journal of Sociology*, 91 (3): 481–510.

Grasmuck, S. and Pessar, P. (1991) *Between Two Islands: Dominican International Migration*, Berkeley, University of California Press.

Gray, Breda (1996) 'The Home of Our Mothers and Our Birthright for Ages? Nation, Diaspora and Irish Women', in Maynard, M. and Purvis, J. (eds) *New Frontiers in Women's Studies*, London, Taylor and Francis.

Green, T. (1981) *The World of Diamonds*, London, Weidenfeld and Nicolson.

Gregson, N. and Lowe, M. (1994) *Servicing the Middle Classes: Class, Gender and Waged Domestic Labour in Contemporary Britain*, London, Routledge.

Groenendijk, K. and Hampsink, R. (1995) *Temporary Employment of Migrants in Europe*, Nijmegen, Reeks Recht and Samenleving.

Guardian, 15 February 1996.

Guardian, 27 January 2000.

Guardian, 24 March 2000: Isabel Fonseca, 'The Truth about Gypsies', pp. 2–3.

Guarnizo, L. E., Sánchez, A. I. and Roach, E. M. (1999) 'Mistrust, Fragmented Solidarity, and Transnational Migration: Colombians in New York City and Los Angeles', *Ethnic and Racial Studies*, 22 (2): 368–95.

Hall, S. (1989) 'New Ethnicities'. Black Film, Black Cinema, ICA Document 7, London, Institute of Contemporary Arts.

—— (1990) 'Cultural Identity and Diaspora', in Rutherford, J. (ed.) *Identity: Community, Culture, Difference*, London, Lawrence and Wishart, pp. 222–37.

—— (1991) 'Old and New Identities, Old and New Ethnicities', in King, A. D. (ed.) *Culture, Globalization and the World-System*, Basingstoke, Macmillan, pp. 48–68.

—— (1992) 'Europe's Other Self: The Challenges of 1992', *The Runnymede Bulletin*, February: 2–3.

Hancock, M. (1983) 'Transnational Production and Women Workers', in Phizacklea, A. (ed.) *One Way Ticket: Migration and Female Labour*, London, Routledge, pp. 113–31.

Harding, S. (ed.) (1987) *Feminism and Methodology*, Milton Keynes, Open University Press.

Harvey, D. (1992) *The Condition of Postmodernity*, Oxford, Blackwell.

Hobsbawm, E. J. (1990) *Nations and Nationalism Since 1780*, Cambridge, Cambridge University Press.

Hoel, B. (1982) 'Contemporary Clothing Sweatshops: Asian Female Labour and Collective Organisation', in West, J. (ed.) *Work, Women and the Labour Market*, London, Routledge.

Hondagneu-Sotelo, Pierette (1995) *Gendered Transitions*, Berkeley, California University Press.

Hoskyns, C. and Orsini-Jones, M. (1994) *Immigrant Women in Italy*, Coventry University.

Huang, C. (1999) 'Management of Migrant Labor in Overseas Chinese Enterprises in South China', *Asian and Pacific Migration Journal*, 8 (3): 361–80.

Hugo, G. (1994) 'Illegal International Migration in Asia', in Cohen, R. (ed.) *The Cambridge Survey of World Migration*, Cambridge, Cambridge University Press, pp. 397–402.

Institute for Race Relations (IRR) (1996) *European Race Audit*, 17 January and 18 March, London, IRR.

Ip, D. and Lever-Tracey, C. (1999) 'Asian Women in Business in Australia', in Gender and Migration (eds) *Gender and Migration*, Basingstoke, Macmillan.

Iris di Rimini (1995) *Immigrati: Pericolo o Risorsa?*, Instituto Ricerche Sociali, Rimini.

Isaacs, A. (1993) *Military Rule and Transition in Ecuador 1972–1992*, London, Macmillan (in association with St Antony's College, Oxford).

Joshi, V. and Little, I. (1996) *India's Economic Reforms 1991–2001*, Oxford, Clarendon Press.

Kanfer, S. (1993) *The Last Empire: DeBeers, Diamonds and the World*, London, Hodder and Stoughton.

Kaur, D. and Hayden, C. (1993) 'Not Just for Pin Money: A Case Study of the West Midlands Clothing Business Start-Up Project', in Allen, S. and Truman, C. (eds) *Women in Business*, London, Routledge.

Kaur, S. (1999) 'Empowering Women Clothing Workers in the West Midlands of Britain', paper presented to the Empowerment of Women in Cotton Textile Industry in India, Karaikudi University, Tamil Nadu, India, 11 March 1999.

Kaye, R. (1997) 'Redefining the Refugee: The UK Media Portrayal of Asylum Seekers', in Koser, K. and Lutz, H. (eds) *The New Migrations in Europe: Social Constructions and Social Realities*, Basingstoke, Macmillan.

Kempadoo, K. (1998) 'Introduction: Globalizing Sex Workers' Rights', in Kempadoo, K. and Doezema, J. (eds) *Global Sex Workers: Rights, Resistance and Redefinition*, London and New York, Routledge, pp. 1–28.

King, A. (ed.) (1991) *Culture, Globalization and the World System*, Binghampton, NY, University of New York Press.

King, R. (1996) *Emancipating Space: Geography, Architecture and Urban Design*, New York, The Guilford Press.

Koser, K. (1997) 'Out of the Frying Pan and Into the Fire: A Case Study of Illegality Amongst Asylum Seekers', in Koser, K. and Lutz, H. (eds) *The*

New Migration in Europe: Social Constructions and Social Realities, Basingstoke, Macmillan, pp. 185–98.

Kyle, D. (1999) 'The Otavalo Trade Diaspora: Social Capital and Transnational Entrepreneurship', *Ethnic and Racial Studies*, 22 (2): 422–56.

Laidlaw, J. (1995) *Riches and Renunciation: Religion, Economy and Society Among the Jains*, Oxford, Oxford University Press.

Lash, S. and Urry, J. (1994) *Economies of Signs and Space*, London, Sage.

Lefebvre, H. (1996) *Writings on Cities* (trans. E. Kofman and E. Labas), Oxford, Blackwell.

Lehman, D. (1996) *Struggle for the Spirit: Religious Transformation and Popular Culture in Brazil and Latin America*, Cambridge, Polity Press.

LIFE (1991) *Filipino Migrant Women in Domestic Work in Italy*, ILO, Geneva.

Lim, L. L and Oishi, N. (1996) 'International Labour Migration of Asian Women: Distinctive Characteristics and Policy Concerns', *Asian and Pacific Migration Journal*, 5 (1): 85–116.

Lindsey, D. (1993) *Body of Truth*, London, Warner Books.

Lovell, N. (ed.) (1999) *Locality and Belonging*, London and New York, Routledge.

MacDonald, J. and MacDonald, L. (1972) *The Invisible Immigrants*, London, Runnymede Trust.

Macklin, Audrey (1994) 'On the Outside Looking In: Foreign Domestic Workers in Canada', in Giles, W. and Arat-Koc, S. (eds) *Maid in the Market*, Halifax, Canada, Fernwood Publishing.

Mallon, F. (1995) *Peasant and Nation: The Making of Postcolonial Mexico and Peru*, Berkeley, University of California Press.

Marr, A. (2000) *The Day Britain Died*, London, Profile Books.

Mars, G. and Ward, R. (1984) 'Ethnic Business Development in Britain', in Ward, R. and Jenkins, R. (eds) *Ethnic Communities in Business*, Cambridge, Cambridge University Press.

Martin-Barbero, J. (1993) *Communication, Culture and Hegemony: From Media to Mediations*, London, Sage.

Martin-Barbero, J. and Muñoz, S. (1992) *Television y Melodrama*, Bogotá, Tercer Mundo Editores.

Mason, T. (1995) *Passion of the People? Football in South America*, London, Verso.

Massey, D. (1993) 'Power-Geometry and a Progressive Sense of Place', in Bird, J. *et al.* (eds) *Mapping the Futures: Local Cultures, Global Change*, New York and London, Routledge, pp. 59–69.

—— (1995) 'Thinking Radical Democracy Spatially', *Environment and Planning: Society and Space*, 13: 283–8.

Massey, D. S. *et al.* (1993) 'Theories of International Migration: A Review and Appraisal', *Population and Development Review*, 19 (3): 432–66.

Meillassoux, C. (1981) *Maidens, Meal and Money*, Cambridge, Cambridge University Press.

Melucci, A. (1989) *Nomads of the Present: Social Movements and Individual Needs in Contemporary Society*, London, Hutchinson.

Menski, W. (1999) 'South Asian Women in Britain, Family Integrity and the Primary Purpose Rule', in Barot, R., Bradley, H. and Fenton, S. (eds) *Ethnicity, Gender and Social Change*, Basingstoke, Macmillan, pp. 81–98.

Migration News Sheet, June 1996 and January 1997, Migration Policy Group, Brussels.

Misztal, B. (1996) *Trust in Modern Societies*, Cambridge, Polity.

Modood, T., Berthoud, R., Lakey, J., Nazroo, J., Smith, P., Virdee, S. and Beishon, S. (1997) *Ethnic Minorities in Britain: Diversity and Disadvantage*, London, Policy Studies Institute.

Morokvasic, M. (1983) 'Women in Migration', in Phizacklea, A. (ed.) *One Way Ticket: Migration and Female Labour*, London, Routledge.

—— (1987) 'Immigrants in the Parisian Garment Industry', *Work, Employment and Society*, 1 (4): 441–62.

—— (1988) *Minority and Immigrant Women in Self-Employment and Business in France, Great Britain, Italy, Portugal and Federal Republic of Germany*, Brussels, Directorate of Social Affairs and Education, CEC.

—— (1991) 'Fortress Europe and Migrant Women', in *Feminist Review*, 39 (Winter): 69–84.

Morokvasic, M., Waldinger, R. and Phizacklea, A. (1990) 'Business on the Ragged Edge: Clothing Entrepreneurs in Paris, London and New York', in Waldinger, R., Aldrich, H. and Ward, R. (eds) *Ethnic Entrepreneurs*, London, Sage.

Mouzelis, N. (1995) *Sociological Theory: What Went Wrong?*, London, Routledge.

Murray, A. (1998) 'Debt-Bondage and Trafficking: Don't Believe the Hype', in Kempadoo, K. and Doezema, J. (eds) *Global Sex Workers*, London and New York, Routledge, pp. 51–65.

Nairn, T. (2000) *After Britain: New Labour and the Return of Scotland*, London, Granta.

Nikolinakos, M. (1975) 'Draft of a General Theory of Migration in Late Capitalism', *Proceedings of International Conference on Migrant Workers*, Berlin, ICSS.

Observer, 26 March 2000, 'Bullet that Tore a Hole in America', p. 23.

OECD (1995) and (1998) *SOPEMI, Trends in International Migration*, Paris, OECD.

Pallister, D., Stewart, S. and Leppe, I. (1987) *South Africa Inc.: The Oppenheimer Empire*, London, Simon and Schuster.

Peach, C. (1968) *West Indian Migration to Britain*, Oxford, Oxford University Press.

Pessar, P. A. (1982) 'The Role of Households in International Migration and the Case of the US Bound Migration from the Dominican Republic', *International Migration Review*, 16 (2), Summer: 342–64

Phillips, A. and Taylor, B. (1980) 'Sex and Skill', *Feminist Review*, 6: 56–79.

Phizacklea, A. (1982) 'Migrant Women and Wage Labour: The Case of West Indian Women in Britain', in West, J. (ed.) *Work, Women and the Labour Market*, London, Routledge.

—— (ed.) (1983) *One Way Ticket: Migration and Female Labour*, London, Routledge.

—— (1987) 'Minority Women and Economic Restructuring: The Case of Britain and the Federal Republic of Germany', *Work, Employment and Society*, 1 (3): 309–25.

—— (1990) *Unpacking the Fashion Industry*, London, Routledge.

—— (1994) 'A Single or Segregated Market?: Gendered and Racialised Divisions', in Afshar, H. and Maynard, M. (eds) *The Dynamics of 'Race' and Gender: Some Feminist Interventions*, London, Taylor and Francis, pp.172–82.

—— (1999) 'Gender and Transnational Labour Migration', in Barot, R., Bradley, H. and Fenton, S. (eds) *Ethnicity, Gender and Social Change*, Basingstoke, Macmillan, pp.29–45.

Phizacklea, A. and Miles, R. (1980) *Labour and Racism*, London, Routledge.

Phizacklea, A. and Ram, M. (1995) 'Ethnic Entrepreneurship in Comparative Perspective', *Entrepreneurial Behaviour and Research*, 1 (1): 48–59.

—— (1996) 'Being Your Own Boss: Ethnic Minority Entrepreneurs in Comparative Perspective', *Work, Employment and Society*, 10 (2): 319–39.

Phizacklea, A and Wolkowitz, C. (1995) *Homeworking Women*, London, Sage.

Pilkington, H. (1997) 'Going Home? The Implications of Forced Migration for National Identity Formation in Post-Soviet Russia', in Koser, K. and Lutz, H. (eds) *The New Migration in Europe: Social Constructions and Social Realities*, Basingstoke, Macmillan, pp. 85–106.

Pilkington, H. and Phizacklea, A. (1999) 'Western Migration Theories and Post-Soviet Migration Practice', in Vyatkin, A., Kosmarskaya, N. and Panarin, S. (eds) *On the Move: Voluntarily and Involuntarily*, Moscow, Natalis Press.

Portes, A. (1997) 'Immigration Theory for a New Century: Some Problems and Opportunities', *International Migration Review*, 31 (4): 799–825.

—— (1999) 'Conclusion: Towards a New World – The Origins and Effects of Transnational Activities', *Ethnic and Racial Studies*, 22 (2): 463–77.

Portes, A., Guarnizo, L. and Landolt, P. (1999) 'The Study of Transnational Communities: Pitfalls and Promise of an Emergent Field', *Ethnic and Racial Studies*, 22 (2): 217–37.

Potts, L. (1990) *The World Labour Market*, London, Zed Press.

Psimmenos, Iordanis (1996) 'The Making of Periphractic Spaces: The Case of Albanian Undocumented Immigrants in Athens City', ECOMER Conference, Utrecht, Netherlands.

Quintero-Lopez, L. (1987) 'El estado terrateniente en el Ecuador (1909–1895)', in Delers, J. P. and Saint-Geours, Y. (eds) *Estados y Naciones en los Andes*, Lima, Instituto de Estudios Peruanos.

Quintero-Lopez, L. and Silva, E. (1991) *Ecuador: Una Nación en Ciernes*, Quito, Ecuador, FLACSO.

Radcliffe, S. (1993) 'The Role of Gender in Peasant Migration: Conceptual Issues from the Peruvian Andes', in Momsen, J. and Kinnaird, V. (eds) *Different Places, Different Voices*, London, Routledge, pp. 278–88.

—— (1996) 'Frontiers and Popular Nationhood – Geographies of Identity in the 1995 Ecuador–Peru Border Dispute', unpublished paper, Department of Geography, University of Cambridge.

Radcliffe, S. and Westwood, S. (1996) *Remaking the Nation: Place, Identity and Politics in Latin America*, London, Routledge.

Ram, M. (1994) *Managing to Survive: Working Lives in Small Firms*, Oxford, Blackwell.

Repack, T. A. (1997) 'New Roles in a New Landscape', in Romero, M. *et al. Challenging Fronteras. Structuring Latina and Latino Lives in the US*, London, Routledge.

Reskin, A. and Padavic, I. (1994) *Women and Men at Work*, Thousand Oaks, California, Pine Forge Press.

Richmond, A. (1988) 'Sociological Theories of International Migration: The Case of Refugees', *Current Sociology*, 36 (2): 7–25.

Roberts, B., Frank, R. and Lozano-Ascensio, F. (1999) 'Transnational Migrant Communities and Mexican Migration to the US', *Ethnic and Racial Studies*, 22 (2): 238–66.

Rowe, W. and Schelling, V. (1991) *Memory and Modernity: Popular Culture in Latin America*, London, Verso.

Rushdie, S. (1999) *The Ground Beneath Her Feet*, London, Jonathan Cape.

Said, E. (1993) *Culture and Imperialism*, London, Chatto and Windus.

Salih, R. (1999) 'Shifting Meanings of "Home": Consumption and Identity in Moroccan Women's Transnational Practices Between Italy and Morocco', paper presented to the New Approaches to Migration Conference, University of Sussex, 21–22 September.

Salt, J. (1988) 'Highly Skilled International Migrants, Careers and Internal Labour Markets', *Geoform*, 19: 87–99.

—— (1992) 'Migration Processes Among the Highly Skilled in Europe', *International Migration Review*, 26: 484–505.

Sassen, S. (1996) 'Analytic Borderlands: Race, Gender and Representation in the New City', in King, A. D. (ed.) *Re-Presenting the City: Ethnicity, Capital and Culture in the 21st Century Metropolis*, London, Macmillan.

Sassen-Koob, S. (1984) 'Notes on the Incorporation of Third World Women into Wage-Labour Through Immigration and Off-Shore Production', *International Migration Review*, 18 (4): 1,144–67.

Sciorra, J. (1996) 'Return to the Future: Puerto Rican Vernacular Architecture in New York City', in King, A. D. (ed.) *Re-Presenting the City: Ethnicity, Capital and Culture in the 21st-Century Metropolis*, London, Macmillan.

Selby, H. and Murphy, A. (1982) *The Mexican Urban Household and the Decision to Migrate to the US*, ISHI Occasional Papers in Social Change, No. 4, Institute for the Study of Human Issues, Philadelphia.

Shohat, E. and Stam, R. (1994) *Unthinking Eurocentrism: Multiculturalism and the Media*, London, Routledge.

Sibley, D. (1995) *Geographies of Exclusion: Society and Difference in the West*, London, Routledge.

Simpson, A. (1993) *Xuxa: The Mega-Marketing of Gender, Race and Modernity*, Philadelphia, Temple University Press.

Singer-Kerel, J. (1980) 'Foreign Labour and the Economic Crisis: The Case of France', paper delivered to the ESF Conference, Akademic Klausenhof, 4123 Hammiinkeln-über-Wessel, 10–12 December.

Skeldon, R. (1999) *Migration of Women in the Context of Globalisation in the Asian and Pacific Region*, Women in Development Discussion Paper Series No. 2, Social Development Division of the ESCAP Secretariat, United Nations.

Smith, A. D. (1991) *National Identity*, London, Penguin.

Smith, D. (1977) *Racial Disadvantage in Britain*, Harmondsworth, Penguin.

Smith, I. (1996) 'After Tompkins Square Park: Degentrification and the Revanchist City', in King, A. D. (ed.) *Re-Presenting the City: Ethnicity, Capital and Culture in the 21st Century Metropolis*, London, Macmillan.

Smith, M. (1999) 'New Approaches to Migration and Transnationalism: Locating Transnational Practices', keynote address given at the conference New Approaches to Migration: Transnational Communities and the Transformation of Home, University of Sussex, UK, 21–22, September.

Soja, E. W. (1997) 'Six Discourses on Postmetropolis', in Westwood, S. and Williams, J. (eds) *Imagining Cities, Scripts, Signs, Memory*, London, Routledge.

SOPEMI (1990) *Continuous Reporting System on Migration*, Paris, OECD (also 1995 and 1998).

Southall Black Sisters (no date) *Domestic Violence and Asian Women*, Southall, Middlesex, UK, Southall Black Sisters.

Stanley, L. and Wise, A. (1983) *Breaking Out: Feminist Consciousness and Feminist Research*, London, Routledge and Kegan Paul.

Stark, O. (1984) 'Migration Decision-Making: A Review Article', *Journal of Development Economics*, 14: 251–9.

—— (1999) *Altruism and Beyond*, Cambridge, Cambridge University Press.

Sunday Times, 'Rich List', 11 April 1999 and 19 March 2000.

Tambs-Lyche, H. (1980) *London Patidars: A Case Study in Urban Ethnicity*, London, Routledge.

Tiano, S. (1994) *Patriarchy on the Line*, Philadelphia, Temple University Press.

Todaro, M. (1969) 'A Model of Labour Migration and Urban Unemployment in Less Developed Countries', *American Economic Review*, 59: 138–48.

—— (1976) *Internal Migration in Developing Countries*, Geneva, ILO.

Truong, Thanh-Dam (1996) 'Gender, International Migration and Social Reproduction: Implications for Theory, Policy, Research and Networking', *Asian and Pacific Migration Journal*, 5 (1): 27–52.

Truong, Thanh-Dam and del Rosario, Virginia (1994) 'Captive Outsiders: Trafficked Sex Workers and Mail-Order Brides in the European Union', in Wiersma, J. (ed.) *Insiders and Outsiders: On the Making of Europe II*, Kampen, Pharos.

Turner, B. (1994) *Orientalism, Postmodernism and Globalism*, London, Routledge.

UNECE (United Nations Economic Commission for Europe) (1995) *International Migration Bulletin*, no. 7 (November).

Urcioli, B. (1997) ' "Official" English as US Cultural Defence Against a Complex World', paper presented at the Globalisation and Ethnicity Conference, Amsterdam.

Urry, J. (2000) *Sociology Beyond Societies: Mobility for the Twenty-First Century*, London, Routledge.

Vertovec, S. (1999) 'Conceiving and Researching Transnationalism', *Ethnic and Racial Studies*, 22 (2): 447–62.

Wade, P. (1993) *Blackness and Race Mixture: The Dynamics of Racial Identity in Colombia*, Baltimore, MD, Johns Hopkins University Press.

—— (1997) *Race and Ethnicity in Latin America*, London, Pluto Press.

Waldinger, R., Aldrich, H. and Ward, R. (eds) (1990) *Ethnic Entrepreneurs*, London, Sage.

Walker, A. and Maltby, T. (1997) *Ageing Europe*, Buckingham, Open University Press.

Walzer, M. (1983) *Spheres of Justice: A Defence of Pluralism and Equality*, Oxford, Blackwell.

Ward, P. M. (1999) *Colonias and Public Policy in Texas and Mexico: Urbanization by Stealth*, Austin, University of Texas Press.

Watson, J. (1977) 'Introduction, Immigration, Ethnicity and Class in Britain', in Watson, J. (ed.) *Between Two Cultures*, Oxford, Blackwell.

Weinert, P. (1991) *Foreign Female Domestic Workers: HELP WANTED!*, Geneva, International Labour Office.

West Rudner, D. (1994) *Caste and Colonialism in Colonial India: The Nattukottai Chettiars*, Los Angeles, University of California Press.

Westwood, S. (1988) 'Workers and Wives', in Westwood, S. and Bhachu, P. (eds) *Enterprising Women*, London, Routledge.

—— (1991) 'Racism, Black Masculinity and the Politics of Space', in Hearn, J. and Morgan, D. (eds) *Men, Masculinity and Social Theory*, London, Unwin and Hyman.

—— (1995) 'Gendering Diaspora: Space, Politics and South Asian Masculinities in Britain', in van der Veer, P. (ed.) *Nation and Migration: The Politics of Space in the South Asian Diaspora*, Philadelphia, PA, University of Pennsylvania Press.

—— (1996) 'Political Love: Nations/National Identities in Latin America', paper presented to the British Sociological Association.

—— (1997) 'Imagining Cities', in Westwood, S. and Williams, J. (eds) *Imagining Cities: Scripts, Signs, Memory*, London, Routledge, pp. 1–16.

Williams, C. and Smith, A. (1983) 'The National Construction of Social Space', *Progress in Human Geography*, 7: 502–18.

Williams, R. (1983) *Towards 2000*, London, Chatto and Windus.

Winant, H. (1992) 'Rethinking Race in Brazil', *Journal of Latin American Studies*, 24 (1): 173–92.

—— (1995) *Racial Conditions: Politics, Theory, Comparisons*, Minneapolis, University of Minnesota Press.

Wood, C. H. (1982) 'Equilibrium and Historical Structural Perspectives on Migration', *International Migration Review*, 16 (2): 298–319.

Yogdev, G. (1978) *Diamonds and Coral: Anglo-Dutch Jews and Eighteenth Century Trade*, Leicester, Leicester University Press.

Zlotnik, Hania (1995) 'The South-to-North Migration of Women', *International Migration Review*, 29 (1): 229–54.

Zukin, S. (1991) *Landscape of Power: From Detroit to Disneyworld*, Berkeley, California, UCLA Press.

Index